Sewing for Children
with African Wax Print Fabric

Sewing for Children
with African Wax Print Fabric

25 stylish and vibrant garments, accessories, and homewares for babies to 5-year-olds

Adaku Parker

CICO BOOKS
LONDON NEW YORK

This book is dedicated to my children.

Published in 2023 by CICO Books
An imprint of Ryland Peters & Small Ltd

20–21 Jockey's Fields   341 E 116th St
London WC1R 4BW   New York, NY 10029

www.rylandpeters.com

10 9 8 7 6 5 4 3 2 1

Text © Adaku Parker 2023
Design, illustration, and photography
© CICO Books 2023

A CIP catalog record for this book is available from
the Library of Congress and the British Library.

ISBN: 978 1 80065 267 5

Printed in China

Editor: Marie Clayton
Designer: Alison Fenton
Photographer: James Gardiner
Stylist: Nel Haynes
Illustrators: Cathy Brear (step-by-step artworks)
and Stephen Dew (templates and
technique artworks)

In-house editor: Jenny Dye
Art director: Sally Powell
Creative director: Leslie Harrington
Head of production: Patricia Harrington
Publishing manager: Penny Craig

FSC
www.fsc.org

MIX
Paper | Supporting
responsible forestry
FSC® C008047

Contents

CHAPTER 1

Accessories 12

CHAPTER 2

Homewares 42

CHAPTER 3

Clothes 54

Introduction

Welcome to my first book of makes for children! These projects combine the art of sewing with the vibrant and culturally rich world of African wax print fabrics. If you're a parent, guardian, carer, or simply someone who loves sewing and wants to create unique and beautiful items for children, then this title is for you.

At the time of writing this book, my own children are aged eight, six, and four. If you have little people in your life, and they are anything like mine, they seem to need new clothes all the time. Here you will find lots of super-simple sewing patterns as well as no-pattern projects that allow you to simply measure, cut, and sew. Suitable for newborns to five-year-olds, the designs will inspire you to embark on a creative journey where you will learn how to incorporate stunning African wax print fabric into your sewing projects for children. Whether you're a beginner or an avid sewer, the book offers a range of patterns, tips, and techniques to help you bring the joy and beauty of this fabric into your sewing repertoire.

African wax print fabric, also known as Ankara fabric, is a colorful and distinctive textile. It is characterized by its bold patterns, vibrant colors, and intricate designs, many telling a story and reflecting the rich heritage of the African continent.

Throughout these pages, you'll discover a variety of adorable and stylish makes specifically designed for children. From dresses and a romper to a shirt, shorts, and accessories, each pattern showcases the versatility of African wax print fabric and provides endless possibilities for your sewing projects. Whether you're sewing for your own children or grandchildren, or making gifts for loved ones, these unique creations are sure to delight and inspire.

Furthermore, the book is designed to be accessible and user-friendly, with detailed instructions, clear illustrations, and helpful tips and tricks. So gather your sewing supplies, select your favorite African wax print fabrics, and join me on this exciting sewing adventure. These projects will help you to create unique, stylish, and culturally inspired garments, accessories, and homewares that celebrate the beauty of African textiles and bring joy to the little people in your life.

African Wax Print Fabric

Origins

"African wax print" describes cotton fabrics that are printed using the industrial wax-resist method. These bold and often brightly-colored textiles feature a range of traditional and contemporary African motifs. The fabrics have an interesting and complex cultural history, and as a result you might hear them being called African Wax Print, Dutch Wax Print, or Ankara Hollandaise.

Cotton has been woven in Africa since the sixth century AD, and would have been printed using natural dyes. However, it was the Dutch that introduced industrially wax-printed cotton designs to the African continent during the early to mid-nineteenth century. At that time, the Netherlands ruled what was then called Dutch East India (present-day Indonesia) and Dutch textile merchants created what we now know as African wax print by imitating the Indonesian Batik print. The traditional Batik method involves hand-painting intricate designs onto cloth using beeswax. Colors are then added to the design and the waxed areas "resist" the penetration of the dye. When the wax is removed, the patterns are revealed.

The Dutch sought to mechanize this process, with a view to mass producing these fabrics and selling them to the Indonesians. Their modernized method involved transferring the design to cylindrical plates (copper rollers) that were covered in wax. These plates then transfered the pattern to both sides of the fabric. This created areas of the fabric, covered in wax, that would "resist" the color penetration. The fabric was then plunged into a vat of indigo dye and the non-waxed areas became bright blue. After some of the wax had been removed, and the fabrics had dried, colors were added one after the other using a stamp or block. It is generally very difficult to produce fabrics that are printed on both sides

with the same pattern and color, so this unique characteristic is something that African wax print manufacturers aspire to achieve and are celebrated for.

The Indonesians, however, were unimpressed with the brighter, graphic wax prints that the Dutch had produced, because the mechanized dyeing process caused a veined or crackling effect that they saw as imperfections. At this time, some 700 soldiers from the Gold Coast in modern day Ghana had returned home from fighting in Java, bringing with them the new fabrics. What the Indonesians had seen as flaws, West Africans considered to be a testament to the quality of the printing process. And so, African wax printing begins in Africa.

Patterns and meanings

For nearly a century, African wax print fabrics contained many Indonesian designs. It wasn't until the early twentieth century that some textile designers began looking to the African continent itself for inspiration, where the motifs are often imbued with social, historical, or cultural meanings.

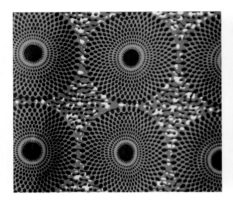

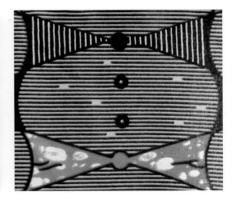

Ripple effect

Also known as "nsubra," meaning waterwell, the circular repeat on this beautiful fabric is supposed to represent a stone being thrown into a well, causing a ripple effect. It is a very popular print and has been reproduced in numerous designs and colorways.

Animals

From horses, chickens, and peacocks to turtles, crocodiles, and butterflies, animals are a recurring theme in African wax print fabrics.

High life

High life literally translates to "living the high life." The motif on this fabric is a bow tie: an accessory often worn with a suit or a tuxedo (dinner jacket) at a black-tie do, symbolizing living the high life.

Sugar cubes

The motifs on this fabric are referred to as sugar cubes because the pattern resembles lumps of sugar still used in Africa today.

The stool

The stool symbol is the key feature of this fabric and its name simply implies, "if you want to talk about me, take a stool and sit down." African proverbs are laden with humorous sayings that also have deeper meanings. If you want to talk about someone, don't just stand around talking. It's better for you to sit down, take your time, and say what you have to say.

Working with African wax print fabric

Preparing your fabric

When working with African wax print fabrics, either for dressmaking, bag making, patchwork, quilting, or upholstery, treat them as you would any medium-weight cotton. The fabric has a stiff, waxy feel to it and will need to be prepared before sewing.

African wax print fabrics come in bolts of either 6 or 12 yards (5.5 or 11 meters), with the manufacturers' stickers or labels on the "right" side of the fabric at one end. These labels can be removed using a steam iron. Place the iron onto the "wrong" side of the fabric and use the steam to soften the industrial glue used to attach the labels. Do this carefully so as not to tear the label and, once the glue is soft, the labels will easily peel away. Do this before you wash the fabric.

To soften the fabric, pre-wash it on a cool (86°F/30°C) wash. When dry, press using the medium steam setting on your iron.

African wax fabric is printed on both sides, so there is little difference between the "right side" and the "wrong side" of the fabric. In order to tell one from the other, you may use the selvage, which is printed with the manufacturer's details and quality statements. On the "right" side, this writing is clearly legible. However, on the "wrong" side, this writing is not decipherable. Before cutting into your fabric, mark the "wrong" side so that you can tell it apart from the "right" side once some or all of the selvage has been cut away. You can either use chalk to mark the wrong side, or use a pin with the head visible on the right side of the fabric.

Pattern matching

Follow these tips when choosing and pattern matching your fabric in order to showcase as much of the African wax print design as possible. See also page 103 for pattern-matching techniques.

◎ Small-scale prints are ideal for garment patterns with multiple smaller pieces, such as shirts, where pattern matching is not as straightforward.

◎ Choose large-scale prints for garment patterns with only a few larger pieces, such as the pinafore dress (see page 86) or a skirt, as cutting into the design multiple times will diminish the impact of a spectacular motif.

◎ For directional designs, those that point in one direction (downward when held one way, upward when turned 180 degrees), cut either on the cross grain or straight grain, depending on the most flattering finish.

◎ Take care that your prints follow the same direction through the garment, such as all pointing downward in bodice, skirt, and sleeves (unless this is a considered part of your design!).

◎ With non-directional prints, find the most economical way of cutting out by placing the pattern pieces as close together as possible.

◎ With large motifs, such as a flower, ensure that the placement of the motif on the front panel is mirrored on the back panel.

◎ When working with larger motifs that require pattern matching, allow extra fabric when purchasing, for example if the pattern suggests 3yd (2.7m) for your size, buy 4yd (3.6m) minimum.

◎ Look for the repeat in the fabric and match that repeat (i.e. the mirror image) so that when you cut out a skirt front and back, for example, the front and the back are identical.

◎ Some African wax prints are printed by hand using block or stamp printing methods and the repeats across the fabric are not always exact. This makes it difficult (although not impossible) to measure a repeat and to pattern match precisely at seams. Instead, why not try to pattern match on the front or back bodice with the motif centered or off-center, with the entirety of the motif contained in one pattern piece or panel.

◎ For the trousers, romper, and shorts, match the outer side seam where possible.

◎ As with all fabrics, cut on the bias when the fabric will be sitting against the neckline, armhole, or wrist. To find the bias, fold one corner of the fabric over until the side that is at right angles to the selvage is lined up with the selvage. The resulting fold line is the bias at 45 degrees to the selvage.

CHAPTER 1

Accessories

This simple item is a must-have for a young baby. The bib pattern is designed to be both practical and stylish, adding a cute touch to baby's outfit while ensuring maximum protection against spills.

Olivia Bib

SIZES
0–3 mth, 3–6 mth, 6–12 mth

FINISHED MEASUREMENTS
0–3 mth: 8⅝ x 11in (22 x 28cm)
3–6 mth: 9⅜ x 11⅜in (24 x 29cm)
6–12 mth: 10 x 12¼in (25.5 x 31cm)

MATERIALS AND TOOLS
2 fat quarters of fabric
1 fat quarter of fusible fleece
Matching sewing thread
1 snap/popper or small piece of hook-and-loop tape
Sewing kit (see pages 100–101)

NOTES
All seam allowances are ⅜in (1cm) unless otherwise stated.

PATTERN PIECE REQUIRED
Bib

1 Pre-wash and "press" your fabric before cutting and sewing (see page 9). Following the manufacturer's instructions, fuse the fleece to the wrong side of one of the bib pieces.

2 Place the fused bib piece and the other bib piece together with the right sides facing. Match up all the edges and pin the two pieces together. Stitch around the edge. Leave a 2in (5cm) gap along the bottom of the bib. Clip notches around the curves (see page 114). This will help the fabric to sit smoothly when the bib is turned right side out.

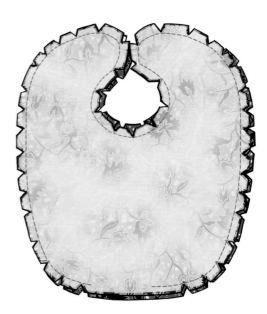

3 Trim the seam allowance down to ¼in (0.5cm) around the entire bib, except at the 2in (5cm) gap in the stitching along the bottom of the bib. Turn the bib right side out through the gap.

4 Tuck in the seam allowance at the gap so that it is flush with the edge of the bib. Press the bib and then pin the gap in place. To close the gap and give the bib a professional finish, topstitch (see page 106) about ⅛in (3mm) in from the edge, all around the edge of the bib. Press. Add a snap fastening following the manufacturer's instructions or hook-and-loop tape to the two top edges of the bib (see page 119).

Alex Drawstring Bag

This fun and functional bag is perfect for carrying toys, books, and snacks on the go. With a simple yet versatile design, it is a great project for sewists of all skill levels. Customize your drawstring bag with a lining of your choice.

DIFFICULTY RATING ◎◎◎

FINISHED MEASUREMENTS
14 x 15¼in (36 x 39cm)

MATERIALS AND TOOLS
½yd (50cm) fabric
½yd (50cm) lining fabric
½yd (50cm) fusible interfacing
Matching sewing thread
2 x 2yd (2m) pieces of string/trim for bag straps
2 eyelets/grommets
Safety pin
Sewing kit (see pages 100–101)

NOTE
All seam allowances are ⅜in (1cm) unless otherwise stated.

CUTTING GUIDE
Cut 2 of the following in each of fabric, lining, and interfacing:
Bag: 16 x 16in (41 x 41cm)

1 Cut the fabric, lining, and interfacing pieces following the cutting guide. Fuse the interfacing pieces (see page 104) to the wrong sides of the main bag fabric pieces.

2 Place the two main fabric pieces together with the right sides facing. Stitch the pieces together along the edges, leaving the top of the bag open. Clip the two bottom corners (see page 115) and press the seams open (see page 113). Repeat for the two lining pieces.

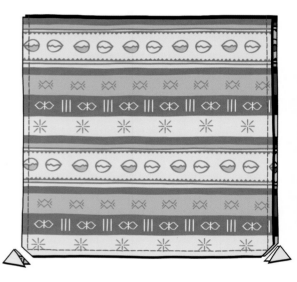

3 Turn the main bag piece inside out, so the right side is on the outside. Slip the lining piece into the main piece so that the wrong sides are together. Make sure the top edges are aligned and the side seams match up. Pin the two pieces together along the top edge. Finish the top of the bag using an overlocker or a zigzag stitch (see page 113).

4 Turn the bag inside out, so the lining is on the outside. Fold the top edge down by 1in (2.5cm) and pin in place. Stitch this in place, ¾in (2cm) down from the folded top edge—this will create the casing for the string. Turn the bag right side out.

5 To make an opening for the string, use a seam ripper to unpick one of the side seams by about ½in (1.5cm), just above the casing stitching line. Make sure that you only go through the top layer of the fabric. Use a zigzag stitch to reinforce the top of the seam so that you only have a small opening. Attach a safety pin to the string and feed it through the casing until you return to the small opening where you started.

6 You will now have the two string ends coming out of the seam at one side of the bag. Cut both ends so that they are 3in (7.5cm) longer than the bag.

7 On the side with the ends of the string, position the eyelets ⅝in (1.5cm) in from the bottom and side of the bag. Attach them following your manufacturer's instructions. Loop one string through the eyelet and tie both ends together in a knot. Repeat steps 5–7 with the other side seam and second piece of string.

David Pencil Case

This practical and fun accessory is perfect for the little people in our lives who need to keep their pencils and markers organized. The roll-up design features multiple pockets and a convenient tie closure, making it easy to take on the go.

DIFFICULTY RATING ◎◎◎

FINISHED MEASUREMENTS
8 x 15in (20.5 x 38cm)

MATERIALS AND TOOLS
24 x 16in (61 x 40.5cm) fabric
Matching sewing thread
20in (50cm) piece of cord
Sewing kit (see pages 100–101)

NOTES
All seam allowances are ⅜in (1cm) unless otherwise stated.

CUTTING GUIDE
Cut 2 of the following in the fabric:
Outer and inner pencil case:
9 x 16in (23 x 40.5cm)

Cut 1 of the following in the fabric:
Pocket: 6 x 16in (15 x 40.5cm)

1 Fold one long edge of the pocket fabric toward the wrong side by ¼in (5mm) and press. Repeat once more, to create a double hem. Sew the hem in place along this long edge.

2 Lay the inner piece right side up and place the pocket piece, also right side, up on top of it. Make sure they are lined up along the sides and bottom edges. Pin in place. Baste-stitch (see page 105) around the sides and bottom edges to keep the pocket piece in place. Create the divisions in the pocket piece by placing a pin 1½in (4cm) in from each side. Then place a pin every 1¼in (3cm) along the top of the pocket in between the two outer pins. Sew a vertical line from top to bottom along the pocket piece where you placed each pin, remembering to backstitch (see page 106) to secure each seam at the beginning and the end.

3 Place the outer piece on top of the inner and pocket pieces with the right sides together. Line up all the sides, and pin in place. Sew around all four sides, leaving a 3in (7.5cm) turning gap along the top edge, and a 1in (2.5cm) gap along one of the short sides, 2¾in (7cm) up from the bottom of the piece, for the cord. Clip the corners (see page 115).

4 Turn the pencil case right side out through the 3in (7.5cm) opening in the top. Tuck under the raw edges of the gaps. Press. Fold the piece of cord in half. Insert the folded end into the 1in (2.5cm) gap in the short side. Pin the cord in place. Topstitch (see page 106) around all four sides, closing the gaps in the top edge and side, and securing the cord in place as you do so.

Francis Fabric Belt

This accessory is perfect for adding a touch of personality to a child's outfit. It's designed to be both functional and fashionable, making it a great addition to any wardrobe.

DIFFICULTY RATING ◎ ◎ ◎

FINISHED MEASUREMENTS
1 x 26in (2.5 x 66cm)

MATERIALS AND TOOLS
3 x 29in (8 x 74cm) fabric
Matching sewing thread
Safety pin
2 x 1½in (4cm) wide D-rings
Sewing kit (see pages 100–101)

NOTES
All seam allowances are ⅜in (1cm) unless otherwise stated.

1 Fold the fabric in half lengthwise with the right sides together. Sew down the long side along the raw edges. To help you turn the piece to the right side, pin a safety pin onto one end of the fabric tube. Push the safety pin inside the tube, and pull and push the safety pin along the tube and out through the other end. Press the belt piece flat.

2 On one end, fold the fabric over by ½in (1.5cm) and then fold it over again by ½in (1.5cm). Sew it in place, close to the inner folded edge.

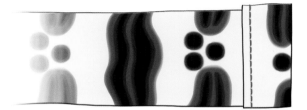

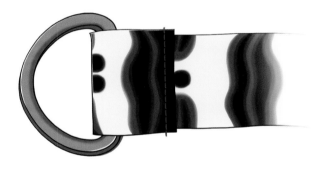

3 Turn the belt over so that you are working on the other side. Fold the end of the belt over by ½in (1.5cm) and press. Slip this end through both of your D-rings. Fold the end of the belt over again by ¾in (2cm). Sew it in place, close to the inner folded edge.

4 To close the belt when it is worn, slide the free end of the belt through both D-rings. Fold this end back on itself, and then slide it over the top D-ring and under the bottom D-ring.

Joseph Tool Belt

This practical and fun accessory is perfect for any young builder or DIY enthusiast. The tool belt features pockets making it easy to carry tools and supplies while keeping hands free.

DIFFICULTY RATING ◎◎◎

FINISHED MEASUREMENTS
8½ x 14in (21.5 x 36cm)

MATERIALS AND TOOLS
14 x 17in (36 x 43cm) fabric
Matching sewing thread
1yd (1m) bias binding, ½in (1.5cm) wide (see page 116 for how to make your own bias binding), cut into three pieces: one measuring 14½in (37cm) and two measuring 10¾in (27.5cm)
1yd (1m) webbing, 1½in (4cm) wide
1¼in (3cm) wide buckle
Sewing kit (see pages 100–101)

1 Fold over one of the short sides of the fabric rectangle by ¼in (0.5cm) toward the wrong side. On this project, it doesn't matter which sides of the fabric you use as the wrong and right side, as both will be showing in the finished belt. Topstitch (see page 106) along the folded edge. Insert the other short side of the rectangle into the fold of the longer strip of bias binding. Stitch close to the inside edge of the bias binding. Snip any excess binding away.

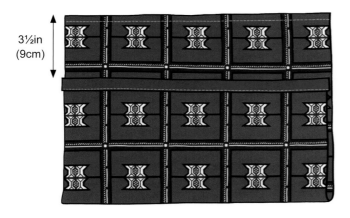

3½in (9cm)

2 Turn the piece over. Fold the bottom of the rectangle up so the bound edge is 3½in (9cm) down from the first finished edge.

3 Open out one of the short bias binding pieces and fold one end under by ⅜in (1cm) toward its wrong side, then refold the binding. Insert one side of the tool belt into the center fold of this bias binding piece, with the folded end of the binding level with the bottom edge of the tool belt. Open out the other end of the binding piece and fold it down toward its wrong side so that the fold is level with the top of the tool belt. This hides the raw ends of the bias binding. Pin in place and repeat on the other side of the tool belt with the other piece of bias binding. Sew the bias binding strips in place close to their inside edges.

4 Turn the tool belt over. Lay the webbing, down so that its top is level with the top of the tool belt. Make sure the tool belt is centered along the webbing.

5 Fold the top of the tool belt, together with the webbing, down. Stitch the strap casing in place along its length by sewing over the original stitch line for the turned-over raw edge that you made at the start.

6 Take one end of the webbing and fold it over by approximately ⅜in (1cm) to the wrong side. Fold it over again by ⅜in (1cm) to enclose the raw edge, and sew it down close to the inside edge. Repeat on the other end of the webbing. On the tool belt, stitch two vertical lines approximately 4¾in (12cm) apart to make the three compartments for the tools. Attach the two sides of the buckle to the ends of the webbing following the manufacturer's instructions.

This cute and practical hat is perfect for keeping your little one warm and stylish. It features a soft and comfortable design, and is suitable for sewists of all skill levels.

Nicole Baby Hat

DIFFICULTY RATING ◎◎◎

SIZES
3–6 mth, 6–12 mth, 12–18 mth

FINISHED MEASUREMENTS
See page 122

MATERIALS AND TOOLS
⅝yd (60cm) fabric, 45in (112cm)
or 60in (152cm) wide
½yd (50cm) lightweight interfacing
Matching sewing thread
1yd (1m) bias binding
Sewing kit (see pages 100–101)

NOTES
All seam allowances are ⅜in (1cm)
unless otherwise stated.

PATTERN PIECES REQUIRED
Front/Back/Side
Brim

1 Cut out the pattern pieces and transfer all pattern markings to the pieces (see page 104). For this hat, you will use six front/back/side pieces for the outer hat: one for the front, one for the back and four for the sides. The remaining sections will be the facing (the inside lining of the hat). The brim is sewn later. With the right sides together, stitch one front section to two side sections using a ¼in (0.5cm) seam allowance. Repeat to stitch one back section to two side sections, to form two halves of the hat. Press the seams open (see page 113).

2 With the right sides facing, pin the two hat sections together. Stitch them together along the outer edge, using a ¼in (0.5cm) seam. This is your side seam. Press this seam open.

3 Repeat steps 1 and 2 with the remaining front, back, and side pieces to make the hat facing.

4 With the wrong sides together, pin the hat facing to the main hat, matching up the seams. To help you do this, you can place a pin through the middle of the corresponding seams on each piece to make sure they are aligned. Baste the raw edges together (see page 105).

5 Apply interfacing to the wrong side of each of the hat brim pieces (see page 104). Stitch the open ends of each of the pieces together. Press the seam open on each piece.

6 With the right sides together, stitch the brim pieces together along the outside edge. Trim and then notch the seam (see page 114).

7 Turn the brim right side out and press. Baste the raw edges together.

8 Working on the outside of the hat, pin the brim to the hat, matching the side seam of the brim to one of the side seams on the hat. Baste the raw edges together. Pin the bias binding all around the raw edge, and then stitch it in place (see page 117).

9 Topstitch (see page 106) close to the bias binding all around the inner edge of the hat.

Joshua Messenger Bag

This stylish messenger bag features a flap closure, a shoulder strap, and plenty of room for storage. It's perfect for storing a small water bottle, snacks, and a favorite small toy.

1 Place the strap pieces together with the right sides facing. Pin together and sew down both of the long sides, leaving the short ends of the strap open.

2 To turn the strap to the right side, pin a safety pin onto one end. Push the safety pin inside the fabric tube, and pull and push the safety pin along the tube and out through the other end. Press the strap and topstitch (see page 106) down both long sides.

3 Lay an outer back piece with the right side facing up and match the strap ends to the straight top edge so they begin ⅜in (1cm) in from each side, with the loop of the strap lying over the back piece. Add an outer flap piece with the right side down, aligning the edges so the strap is sandwiched between the layers. Sew along the straight edge only, securing the strap ends in place. Repeat with the lining back and flap piece, without the strap. Open out both pieces flat and press the seam allowance toward the bag.

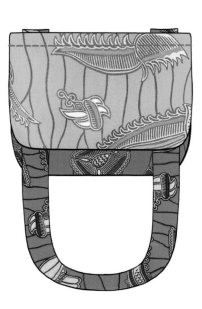

DIFFICULTY RATING ◎ ◎ ◎

FINISHED MEASUREMENTS
7 x 8⅝in (18 x 22cm)

MATERIALS AND TOOLS
½yard (50cm) fabric (in this project I have used African wax print for the outer bag and lining, but you may wish to use a contrasting fabric for the lining)
Matching sewing thread
Safety pin
Sewing kit (see pages 100–101)

NOTES
All seam allowances are ⅜in (1cm) unless otherwise stated.

CUTTING GUIDE
Cut 2 x Front/Back on fold (2 for the outer bag and 2 for the lining)
Cut 2 x Flap on fold (1 for the outer bag and 1 for the lining)
Cut 2 for the strap:
4 x 38in (10 x 97cm) strip

TEMPLATE PIECES REQUIRED
Front/Back
Flap

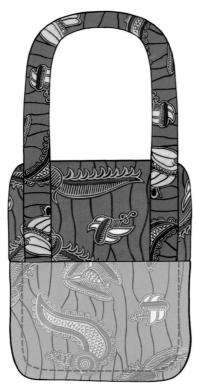

4 Lay the outer front piece onto the outer back piece with right sides facing. Line up and sew around the sides and bottom of the front piece, making sure not to catch the strap in the seam. Repeat with the lining front and back piece, leaving a 3in (7.5cm) gap in the bottom seam.

5 Tuck the strap down inside the outer bag so that it doesn't get caught in the stitching. Turn the lining right side out and insert it into the outer bag.

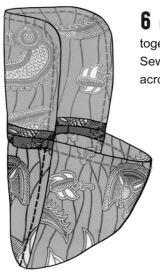

6 Line up and pin the outer bag and lining together along the flap and top of the bag front. Sew the pieces together around the flap and across the top of the bag front.

7 Pull the bag right side out through the gap in the lining. Sew the gap closed and then push the lining back inside the bag. Topstitch (see page 106) around the flap to finish.

This adorable accessory is ideal for keeping your little one's hair out of their face. It is designed to be comfortable while also adding a pop of color and style to their outfit. Why not mix and match prints by using one design on one side and a different print on the other: a perfect stash-busting idea.

Ruby Head Tie

DIFFICULTY RATING ◎◎◎

SIZES

0–3 mth, 3–6 mth, 6–12 mth, 12–18 mth, 18–24 mth, 2–3 yr, 3–4 yr, 4–5 yr

FINISHED MEASUREMENTS

See page 122

MATERIALS AND TOOLS

1 fat quarter fabric

Matching sewing thread

9in (23cm) of 1in (2.5cm) wide elastic

Safety pin

Sewing kit (see pages 100–101)

NOTES

All seam allowances are ⅜in (1cm) unless otherwise stated.

CUTTING GUIDE

Cut 4 x Head Tie

Cut 2 strips, each measuring 1⅞ x 18in (4.7 x 46cm)

TEMPLATE PIECE REQUIRED

Head tie

1 Pre-wash and "press" your fabric before cutting and sewing (see page 9). Place two of the head tie pieces together with the right sides facing. Pin and then stitch together, leaving the short straight side unstitched. Trim the seam allowance in half. Repeat with the other two head tie pieces. Turn both pieces right side out.

2 Place the two strips of fabric together with the right sides facing. Pin and then stitch together, leaving the short sides unstitched. Turn the piece right side out and press. Pin one end of the elastic to a safety pin and thread it through the back piece. Remove the safety pin. Align one end of the elastic with the raw edges of one short side of the back piece. Pin in place and secure using zigzag stitch (see page 113). Repeat to secure the other end of the elastic to the other short side of the back piece.

3 Tuck under the raw edges of the two head tie pieces by ⅜in (1cm) and press. Insert each end of the back piece into each end of the head tie pieces. Pin and then topstitch each end in place (see page 106).

Billie Soft Crib Shoes

These cloth shoes are soft on your baby's delicate feet, while also providing a snug fit to keep them secure. Making your own crib shoes is not only a fun project, but also allows you to create something unique and special for your little one.

DIFFICULTY RATING ◎◎◎

SIZES
0–3 mth, 3–6 mth,
6–9 mth, 9–12 mth

FINISHED MEASUREMENTS
See page 122

MATERIALS AND TOOLS
1 fat quarter fabric
1 fat quarter lining fabric
1 fat quarter interfacing
½in (1.3cm) wide elastic—see cuttting guide for length required
Matching sewing thread
Safety pin
Sewing kit (see pages 100–101)

NOTE
All seam allowances are ⅜in (1cm) unless otherwise stated.

1 Pre-wash and "press" your fabric before cutting and sewing (see page 9). Transfer all pattern markings to the pieces (see page 104). Fuse the interfacing pieces to the main top and main sole pieces, following the manufacturer's instructions.

2 Take one heel main piece and one heel lining piece and place them together with the right sides facing, lining up the edges. Sew the pieces together along the straight top edge.

3 Turn the heel and lining piece to the right side and press. Topstitch along the top edge, ⅟₁₆in (2mm) away from the pressed fold (see page 106). Next, sew a straight line, ½in (1.3cm) below the first stitch line to make a casing for the elastic.

PATTERN PIECES REQUIRED
Heel
Sole (when cutting the sole pieces, flip the pattern for the second piece of main, lining, and interfacing fabrics so you have a left and right sole)
Top

CUTTING GUIDE FOR ELASTIC
Length required of ½in (1.3cm) wide elastic for each size:
0–3 mth: 8½in (21.5cm)
3–6 mth: 8½in (21.5cm)
6–9 mth: 9in (23cm)
9–12 mth: 9in (23cm)

4 Take the required length of elastic for the age of the child as per the cutting guide and cut it into two equal halves. Pin a safety pin to one end of one of the elastic pieces and thread it through the casing in one of the heel pieces. Remove the safety pin. Secure the ends of the elastic on both sides by sewing back and forth a few times (see step 2 on page 36). Repeat steps 2–4 with the other heel piece, heel lining, and elastic.

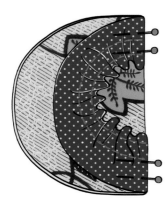

5 Next, you will attach the heel piece to the main top piece. With the right sides together, line up the straight shorter edges of the heel piece with the straight edge of the main top piece and pin in place. Note that the edge of the heel piece with the elastic faces the straight edge.

6 Place the top lining piece, right side down, on top of the main top and heel piece. Pin in place. Sew along the straight edge.

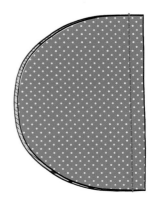

7 Turn the lining over to the right side and pull out the heel piece tight. You will see that your bootie has started to take shape. If desired, you can topstitch (see page 106) along the straight edge of the top piece.

8 Next, you will attach the sole lining to the top of the bootie. Place the sole lining on your work surface with the right side facing upward. Place the top of the bootie, wrong side down, on top of the sole lining and pin in place. Sew all around the edge using a ¼in (6mm) seam allowance, removing the pins as you go.

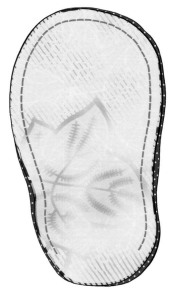

9 Next, you will attach the main sole piece. Place the main sole piece over the top piece, with the right sides together. Pin. Sew all around the edge, leaving a gap of about 1½in (4cm).

10 Pull the fabric out through the gap to turn the bootie to the right side. Tuck under the raw edges of the gap neatly and slip stitch (see page 105) the gap closed. Repeat steps 5–10 to make the second bootie.

CHAPTER 2

✳✳✳

Homewares

Ben Storage Bucket

As parents and carers, we all know how quickly toys can take over our homes. This bucket is a practical storage solution and also a great way to add a pop of color and fun to your child's room. They'll love being able to organize their toys, and you'll love the clutter-free look of your home.

DIFFICULTY RATING

FINISHED MEASUREMENTS
Height: 12in (30.5cm)
Width at base: 5½in (14cm)

MATERIALS AND TOOLS
½yd (50cm) outer fabric
½yd (50cm) lining fabric
½yd (50cm) heavyweight fusible interfacing
Matching sewing thread
Sewing kit (see pages 100–101)

NOTES
All seam allowances are ¼in (6mm), unless stated otherwise.

✳✳✳✳✳✳✳✳✳✳✳✳✳✳✳✳

CUTTING GUIDE
Cut 2 of the following in each of outer fabric, lining, and interfacing:
Bucket: 17 x 17in (43 x 43cm)

✳✳✳✳✳✳✳✳✳✳✳✳✳✳✳✳

1 Pre-wash and "press" your fabric before cutting and sewing (see page 9). Iron the interfacing squares onto the backs of the outer squares following the manufacturer's instructions.

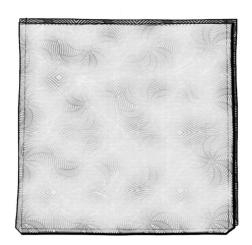

2 Pin the outer squares together with the right sides facing. Sew along three of the four edges. Clip the bottom two corners (see page 115). Repeat to sew the two lining pieces together.

3 Next, you will create boxed corners to give the storage bucket volume and stability. Hold one of the corners on the outer piece, and from the inside, push your finger into the corner and flatten it to make a triangle. Make sure that the seams on each side of the triangle are lined up. Pin in place. Use a ruler and pencil to draw a line that is 3½in (9cm) away from the point of the triangle. Sew along this line. Cut away the excess fabric, leaving a ¼in (6mm) seam allowance. Repeat for the remaining corner on the outer piece, and for the two corners on the lining piece.

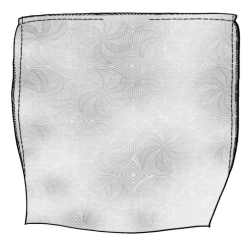

4 Turn the lining piece right side out, but keep the outer piece wrong side out. Insert the lining piece into the outer piece so that the right sides are together. Pin in place. Sew all around the top edge, leaving a 4in (10cm) turning gap on one side. This is where you will turn the bucket right side out in the next step.

5 Pull the fabric through the gap to turn the bucket right side out. Tuck under the raw edges of the turning gap and pin in place. Press the top edge of the bucket. Topstitch (see page 106) around the top of the bucket, ⅛in (3mm) from the edge. You will close the gap as you sew.

Charlene Envelope Pillow

A pillow is a versatile home decor item that will add comfort and style to a child's room or nursery. This simple project is suitable for sewers of any skill level.

DIFFICULTY RATING

FINISHED MEASUREMENTS
20 x 20in (51 x 51cm)*

MATERIALS AND TOOLS
21 x 46in (53.5 x 117cm) fabric*
Matching sewing thread
20 x 20in (51 x 51cm) pillow form (cushion pad)*
Sewing kit (see pages 100–101)

NOTES
All seam allowances are ⅜in (1cm) unless otherwise stated.

*See step 1 and cutting guide if you would like to make a pillow in a different size

1 Pre-wash and "press" your fabric before cutting and sewing (see page 9). If you would like to make a cover for a pillow form that is a different size to the ones in the cutting guide, first measure the height and width of your pillow form. Make sure you are measuring around the curve of your pillow. Use the following formula to measure and cut a rectangular piece of fabric in the correct size for your pillow.

Fabric width: Add 1in (2.5cm) to the height of the cushion, to allow for the seam allowance.

Fabric length: Multiply the width x 2 (for the back and front) and then add 6in (15.5cm). Reduce the length by 1in (2.5cm) if you want a tight-fitting pillow cover.

CUTTING GUIDE FOR COMMON PILLOW SIZES

Cut 1 rectangle in the fabric with the following length and width:

Pillow-form size	14 x 14in (36 x 36cm)	16 x 16in (40 x 40cm)	18 x 18in (45 x 45cm)	20 x 20in (50 x 50cm)
Fabric width	15in (38cm)	17in (43cm)	19cm (48.5cm)	21in (53.5cm)
Fabric length	34in (86.5cm)	38in (96.5cm)	42in (107cm)	46in (117cm)

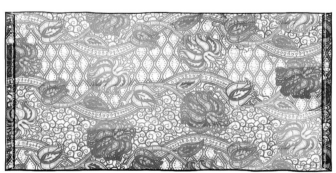

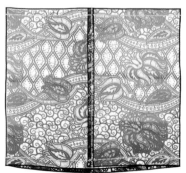

2 With your fabric wrong side up, fold the short sides over by ¼in (6mm) and press. Fold these sides over again by ¼in (6mm) and press. Stitch along the hems, ⅜in (1cm) away from the folded edges.

3 With the right sides together, fold in the left and right hemmed edges so that they overlap by 3½in (9cm), making sure that the overlap is centered. Sew along the top and bottom raw edges. Clip the corners (see page 115). Turn the pillow cover the right way out through the opening, and give it a good press. Insert the cushion form.

Perfect for novice sewers, this toy bag is a simple and easy way to add a touch of style to a child's bedroom decor. Choose from a variety of fabrics, colors, and patterns to make a bold statement.

✳✳

Noah Toy Bag

DIFFICULTY RATING ◎◎◎◎

FINISHED MEASUREMENTS
23 x 30in (58.5 x 76cm) (with the faux trim pressed away from the opening)

MATERIALS AND TOOLS
Fabric, 36 x 42in (92 x 107cm)
Matching sewing thread
Point turner or chopstick (optional)
Sewing kit (see pages 100–101)

NOTE
All seam allowances are ½in (1.3cm) unless otherwise stated.

1 Pre-wash and "press" your fabric before cutting and sewing (see page 9). Fold the fabric in half with the right sides together, so that you get a rectangle that is approximately 21 x 36in (53.5 x 92cm). Pin along the raw long edge and one of the short sides. Stitch along these two sides. Clip the corner to reduce the bulk (see page 115).

2 Finish the raw edges of the seam with a zigzag stitch (see page 113) or an overlocker. Place the opening of the bag over the end of an ironing board. Fold the top edge of the bag toward the wrong side by 4½in (11.5cm) and press. Fold the top edge of the bag to the wrong side again by 4½in (11.5cm) and press. With the bag still inside out, stitch all around the opening of the bag, ½in (1.3cm) away from the folded edge.

3 Turn the bag right side out. Use a point turner or chopstick to push the corners out, and press flat. Press the faux trim piece toward the main bag, or away from the opening, as you prefer.

Eve Baby Changing Mat

This project shows you how to create a portable changing mat for your little one. You may want to place a baby muslin cloth on top of the waterproof layer before use. It's easy to fold up and store in your diaper bag or car.

DIFFICULTY RATING ◎◎◎

FINISHED MEASUREMENTS
24 x 24in (61 x 61cm)

MATERIALS AND TOOLS
1½yd (1.4m) fabric
¾yd (75cm) fusible fleece
¾yd (75cm) vinyl
Matching sewing thread
Sewing kit (see pages 100–101)
Walking foot (this will help you to sew over the bulky seams in this project)

NOTES
All seam allowances are ⅜in (1cm) unless otherwise stated.

CUTTING GUIDE
Cut 2 of the following in the fabric and 1 each in the fusible fabric and vinyl:
Changing mat: 24 x 24in (61 x 61cm)

Cut 4 of the following in fabric:
Pleated border: 6 x 45in (15 x 115cm)

1 Cut the fabric, fusible fleece, and vinyl pieces following the cutting guide. Fuse the fleece to the wrong side of one of the main fabric squares.

2 To make the pleated border, first make a piece of fabric that measures 6in x approx. 5yd 8in (15cm x approx. 4.8m). To do this, place two of the strips you cut for the binding together with their right sides facing, and sew along one of the short edges. Repeat to sew the remaining two strips to this piece, to create one long strip of fabric.

3 Fold the strip of fabric in half along its length, with the right sides together. Baste (see page 105) in place along the raw edges to create a 3in (7.5cm) wide strip of fabric.

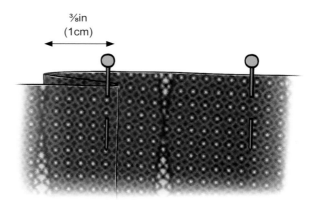

4 To make knife pleats along your 3in (7.5) wide strip of fabric, first measure 4in (10cm) from one end of the strip, and place a pin there to leave an unpleated tail. Mark the fabric with pins or chalk every 2½in (6.5cm) along the folded edge, starting at the 4in (10cm) point. These are the points where the pleats will be folded. Fold the fabric at the first pin, press it down about ⅜in (1cm) away from the pin, and pin in place. This is your first pleat. Repeat along the entire length of the strip until you have a pleated strip. Leave a short tail at the other end.

5 Press the pleats and baste in place along the raw edge, using a ¼in (6mm) seam allowance. Remove the pins.

6 Pin the pleated strip to the edges of the fabric square that has not been fused to the fleece. Make sure that you line up the raw edge of the pleated strip with the four raw edges of the outer piece. Leave the tails unpinned at one corner. Fold the edge of one of the tails under itself to hide the raw edge. Trim the other tail if necessary, and place it under the other folded tail to hide the raw edge. Pin in place. Baste-stitch the strip to the fabric square using a ¼in (6mm) seam allowance.

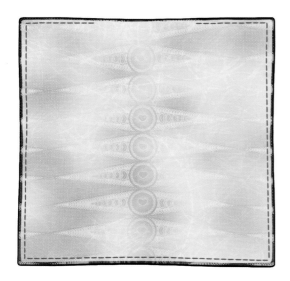

7 With the pleats still facing upward, lay the vinyl on top of the fabric piece. Then lay the fleeced outer piece on top of the vinyl with the fleeced side facing upward. Stitch around all four sides using a 1½in (4cm) seam allowance. Leave a 10in (25.5cm) gap along one edge. Clip the corners and trim the seams (see page 115).

8 Turn the changing mat through to the right side through the gap. Tuck in the raw edges of the gap on both sides of the mat. Edge-stitch to close the 10in (25.5cm) gap.

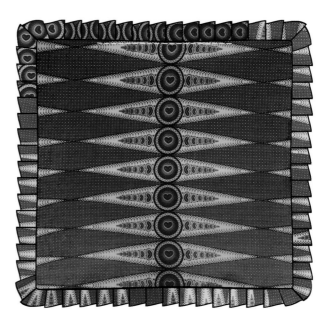

CHAPTER 3

Clothes

Amelia Bloomers

Make these bloomers for your own little one or as a thoughtful gift. This pattern is a comfortable and adorable garment that's perfect for warm weather, and will keep your baby cool and stylish all season long.

DIFFICULTY RATING

SIZES
6–9 mth, 9–12 mth, 12–18 mth, 18–24 mth

FINISHED MEASUREMENTS
See page 122

MATERIALS AND TOOLS
½yd (50cm) fabric, 45in (112cm) or 60in (152cm) wide

Matching sewing thread

½in (1.3cm) wide elastic (see cutting guide for length)

¼in (6mm) wide elastic (see cutting guide for length)

Safety pin

Sewing kit (see pages 100–101)

NOTE
All seam allowances are ⅜in (1cm) unless otherwise stated.

PATTERN PIECES REQUIRED
Front
Back

CUTTING GUIDE FOR ELASTIC

Length required of ½in (1.3cm) wide elastic for each size:	Length required of ¼in (6mm) wide elastic for each size:
6–9 mth: 17¼in (44cm)	6–9 mth: 2 x 9in (23cm) pieces
9–12 mth: 18¼in (46.5cm)	9–12 mth: 2 x 9½in (24cm) pieces
12–18 mth: 19in (48.5cm)	12–18 mth: 2 x 10in (25.5cm) pieces
18–24 mth: 19¼in (49cm)	18–24 mth: 2 x 10¼in (26cm) pieces

1 Pre-wash and "press" your fabric before cutting and sewing (see page 9). Cut out the pieces, pattern matching if necessary (see page 103). Lay the front piece on the back piece with the right sides together. Pin together along the side seams and the crotch. Stitch the side seams and crotch seam.

2 To make the casings for the elastic, along the top edge, turn the fabric over by ¼in (6mm) to the wrong side and press. Turn this edge over to the wrong side again by 1½in (4cm) and press. Topstitch (see page 106) around this edge, ¾in (2cm) from the upper edge, leaving a 2in (5cm) gap in the seam (this is where you will insert the elastic later). Turn each of the leg openings under by ⅜in (1cm) to the wrong side and press. Turn these edges over to the wrong side again by ⅜in (1cm) to the wrong side and press. Topstitch close to the inside edges of the leg hems, leaving a 2in (5cm) gap in each side.

3 Fix a safety pin to one end of your ½in (1.3cm) wide elastic. Feed it into the opening in the waistline, through the casing, and back out the other side of the opening. Overlap the ends of the elastic by ¾in (2cm) and stitch them together using zigzag stitch (see step 3 on page 59). Stretch the waist so the elastic goes into the casing. Topstitch the casing opening closed. Repeat this step for each of the legs, this time using your two pieces of ¼in (6mm) wide elastic.

Whether these shorts will be worn at the beach, playground, or just while hanging out at home, this pattern is perfect for creating a comfortable and stylish garment that your child will love to wear all summer long. The elasticated waistband makes it a perfect project for beginners.

Sydney Shorts

DIFFICULTY RATING

SIZES
2–3 yr, 3–4 yr, 4–5 yr

FINISHED MEASUREMENTS
See page 122

MATERIALS AND TOOLS
1yd (1m) fabric, 45in (112cm)
or 60in (152cm) wide
Matching sewing thread
24in (61cm) of ¼in (6mm)
wide elastic
Safety pin
Sewing kit (see pages 100–101)

PATTERN PIECES REQUIRED
Front/Back

NOTE
All seam allowances are ⅜in (1cm)
unless otherwise stated.

1 Pre-wash and "press" your fabric before cutting and sewing (see page 9). Cut out the pieces, pattern matching if necessary (see page 103). Place the two shorts pieces together with their right sides facing. Stitch them together along the rise and seat. Finish these edges with zigzag stitch or an overlocker (see page 113).

2 Finish the hems and inside leg edges of the shorts using zigzag stitch or an overlocker. With the right sides together, stitch the inside leg seams.

3 Turn the waist to the wrong side by ¼in (6mm) and then again by 1in (2.5cm). Topstitch (see page 106) around the waist, ⅝in (1.5cm) down from the top edge, and leaving a 2in (5cm) gap. Cut the ¼in (6mm) wide elastic so that it measures the circumference of the child's waist minus 2in (5cm). Pin one end of the elastic to a safety pin and insert it through the gap. Thread the elastic through casing. Make sure the elastic isn't twisted inside the casing. Overlap and pin both ends of the elastic together where they emerge through the gap. Stitch the ends of the elastic together with a few rows of zigzag stitching.

4 Stretch the waist so the elastic goes into the casing. Topstitch the 2in (5cm) gap on the waist closed. Turn the hem on each leg to the wrong side by ⅜in (1cm) and topstitch it in place close to the overlocked or zigzag-stitched edge.

Adora Dress

The button or popper closure on this classic dress makes it easy to put on and take off, while the sleeveless design is perfect for warm weather. Pair with a long-sleeve top as the weather cools.

DIFFICULTY RATING ◎◎◎

SIZES

6–9 mth, 9–12 mth, 12–18 mth, 18–24 mth

FINISHED MEASUREMENTS

See page 123

MATERIALS AND TOOLS

1yd (1m) fabric, 45in (112cm) or 60in (152cm) wide

Matching sewing thread

7 x ½in (1.3m) wide snaps/poppers or buttons

1yd (1m) bias binding

Sewing kit (see pages 100–101)

NOTES

All seam allowances are ⅜in (1cm) unless otherwise stated.

PATTERN PIECES REQUIRED

Bodice Front

Bodice Back

Skirt Front

Skirt Back

Patch pocket

1 Pre-wash and "press" your fabric before cutting and sewing (see page 9). Cut out the pieces, pattern matching if necessary (see page 103). Transfer all pattern markings to the pieces (see page 104).

2 Lay the front pieces onto the back piece with the right sides together. Stitch the shoulder seams and side seams. Finish the seams using zigzag stitch (see page 113) or an overlocker.

3 Lay the skirt front pieces onto the skirt back piece with the right sides together, matching up the side seams. Pin and then stitch the side seams. Finish the seams with zigzag stitch or an overlocker. Press the side seams toward the back skirt piece.

4 To gather the upper edge of the skirt, sew two lines of gathering stitches in between the crosses (see Tips on page 109). Follow steps 2–5 on pages 108–109 to gather this edge and stitch the upper edge of the skirt to the lower edge of the bodice with the right sides together. Finish the seam with zigzag stitch, or with an overlocker, and press toward the top of the dress.

5 Place two pocket pieces together with the right sides facing, matching up the edges. Pin together. Stitch around the edges, leaving a 1½in (4cm) gap at the bottom. Repeat with the other two pocket pieces.

6 Turn each pocket piece through to the right side through the gap. Press. Follow the markings on the skirt front pieces to pin each pocket piece in place on the right sides of the skirt fronts. Topstitch (see page 106) the pockets in place around the sides and bottom edges, leaving the upper edges of the pockets unstitched.

7 To hem the lower edge of the skirt, fold this edge to the wrong side of the fabric by ⅜in (1cm) and press. Fold it over to the wrong side of the fabric again by ⅜in (1cm) and press. Topstitch the hem in place, ¼in (6mm) from the bottom edge of the skirt.

8 Following the marked notches on the center fronts of the dress, fold the edge of each placket (button stand) over to the wrong side to the first notch and press. Fold it over again to the second notch and press. Beginning about 2in (5cm) up from the bottom of the skirt, stitch down one side of each placket across the bottom and up the other side in a U shape, to secure the plackets in place. Follow the manufacturer's instructions to attach the front pieces of the snaps to the right-hand-side placket (when worn), and the bottom pieces of the snaps to the left-hand-side placket. Position the snaps so they are evenly spaced.Alternatively, you can sew buttons on the left-hand-side placket and buttonholes on the right-hand-side placket (see pages 118–119).

9 Attach bias binding to finish the neckline and sleeve edges (see page 117).

Stirling Shirt

Whether you're looking to make a shirt for your child's everyday wear or for a special occasion, this pattern has got you covered. You could mix and match prints across the pieces to create a truly unique garment.

DIFFICULTY RATING ◎◎◎

SIZES
2–3 yr, 3–4 yr, 4–5 yr

FINISHED MEASUREMENTS
See page 123

MATERIALS AND TOOLS
1yd (1m) fabric, 45in (112cm) or 60in (152cm) wide
20in (50cm) lightweight fusible interfacing
Matching sewing thread
4 x ⅜in (1cm) snaps/poppers or buttons
Sewing kit (see pages 100–101)

NOTES
All seam allowances are ⅜in (1cm) unless otherwise stated.

PATTERN PIECES REQUIRED
Front
Back
Front Facing
Back Facing
Collar
Sleeve
Sleeve Band

1 Pre-wash and "press" your fabric before cutting and sewing (see page 9). Cut out the pieces, pattern matching if necessary (see page 103). Transfer all pattern markings to the pieces (see page 104).

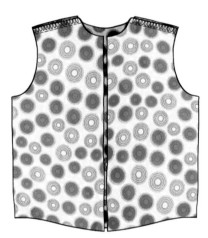

2 With the right sides together, place the two front pieces onto the back piece, matching the raw edges at the shoulders. Stitch the shoulder seams. Finish the raw edges of the shoulder seams using zigzag stitch (see page 113) or an overlocker.

3 Apply lightweight fusible to the wrong side of one of the collar pieces (this will be the under collar). With the right sides together, pin and sew the upper collar section to the matching under collar section, leaving the shorter curve open (see page 111). Trim the seam and clip the curve (see page 114). Turn the collar to the right side and press.

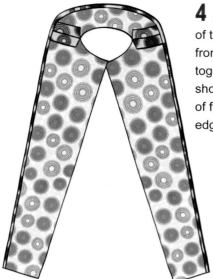

4 Apply the lightweight interfacing to the wrong side of both of the front facing pieces and the back facing piece. Place the front facings onto the back facing piece with the right sides together, matching the raw edges at the shoulders. Stitch the shoulders and press the seams open. Turn the outer raw edge of facings toward the wrong side by ⅛in (3mm). Press these edges and stitch them close to the folded edge.

5 With the wrong side of the under collar facing toward the right side of bodice, pin and baste (see page 105) the collar to the neckline, matching the ends of the collar to the notches on the shirt fronts and using a ¼in (6mm) seam allowance.

6 With the right sides together, pin the facing to the bodice, matching the neckline raw edges. Stitch along the two center fronts and the neckline. Trim the seams and clip the corners (see page 115). Fold the facing to the inside of the shirt, allowing the seamline to roll just to the inside. Press in place.

7 Understitch the facing to the neckline (see page 110). Use hand stitches to secure the facing side seams to the shoulders.

8 With the right sides together, pin one sleeve piece into one of the armholes, matching the notches. Stitch together along the raw edges. Press the seam allowance toward the sleeve. Finish the raw edges of the sleeve seam allowance using zigzag stitch or an overlocker. Repeat with the other sleeve.

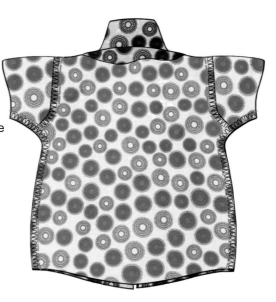

9 With the right sides together, stitch the front, back, and sleeve side seam on each side. Press the seams toward the back of the shirt. Finish the raw edges using zigzag stitch or an overlocker.

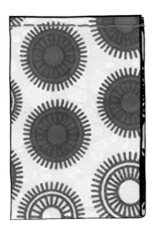

10 Fold one of the cuff pieces in half with the right sides together, matching up the two short edges. Pin and stitch the cuff at the short edge. Press the seam open (see page 113).

11 Open out the cuff, and fold one edge down toward the other edge, with the wrong sides together.

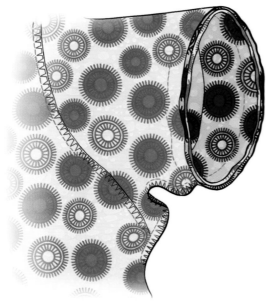

12 With the right sides together, insert the cuff into the sleeve, lining up the raw edges and matching the seams. Pin and then stitch in place. Finish the seam using zigzag stitch or an overlocker. Turn the cuff downward, out of the sleeve, and press the seam toward the sleeve.

13 Fold the raw edge of the shirt hem under by ¼in (6mm) and press. Fold the edge over by another ¼in (6mm), enclosing the raw edge, and press. Topstitch (see page 106) the hem close to the inner folded edge.

14 Mark the positions of the snaps so they are evenly spaced down the front opening. Following the manufacturer's instructions, attach the tops of the snaps to the left-hand side (when worn) of the shirt, and the bottoms of the snaps to the right-hand side. Alternatively, you can sew buttonholes and buttons (see pages 118–119). For boys, buttonholes are on the right-hand side of the shirt and buttons on the left (when worn).

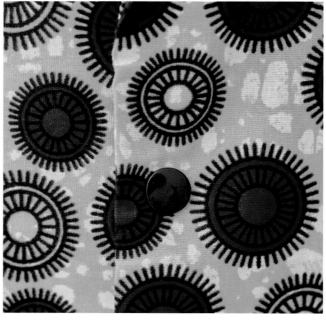

Not only is making your own waistcoat a fun and rewarding project, but it also allows you to create a unique and personalized piece for your child. Whether it's for a wedding, a formal event, or just for everyday wear, this waistcoat will add a touch of charm to any outfit.

Zachary Waistcoat

DIFFICULTY RATING ◎ ◎ ◎

SIZES
2–3 yr, 3–4 yr, 4–5 yr

FINISHED MEASUREMENTS
See page 123

MATERIALS AND TOOLS
1yd (1m) fabric, 45in (112cm)
or 60in (152cm) wide
1yd (1m) fabric, 45in (112cm)
or 60in (152cm) wide
2 x ¾in (2cm) buttons
Matching sewing thread
Sewing kit (see pages 100–101)

NOTES
All seam allowances are ⅜in (1cm)
unless otherwise stated.

PATTERN PIECES REQUIRED
Front
Back
Welt Pocket
Patch Pocket

1 Pre-wash and "press" your fabric before cutting and sewing (see page 9). Cut out all the pieces, pattern matching if necessary (see page 103).

2 Transfer the button and upper pocket markings to the right side of the fabric on the left-hand-side main front piece (when worn). Transfer the welt pocket markings to the outside of the waistcoat front pieces and to the wrong side of the welt pocket pieces. Transfer the dart markings to the wrong sides of the main and lining waistcoat fronts.

3 Optional step: Trim the patch pocket lining and the front and back waistcoat lining pieces by ⅛in (3mm) all around. This will make the lining ever so slightly smaller than the main fabric, and result in the seams rolling toward the lining when the waistcoat is finished, making for an overall neater appearance. This also makes the edges easier to press.

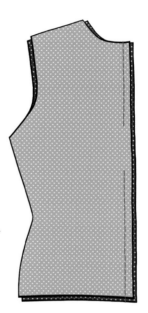

4 Place the two waistcoat back lining pieces together with their right sides facing. Sew the center back seam using a ¼in (6mm) seam allowance, leaving a 2in (5cm) gap in the middle of the seam for turning the waistcoat right side out later.

5 Pin the darts in the waistcoat front and lining pieces. Sew the darts using the dart marking lines as a guide (see page 107).

6 Place the welt pocket pieces onto the waistcoat fronts with the right sides together. Match the welt markings on both pieces (place pins through the corners to do this). Stitch the welt pocket outer line, stopping with the needle down to pivot at the corners. Cut both pieces of fabric along the cutting line in the center. Cut as close as possible into the corners, taking care not to cut through the stitch line.

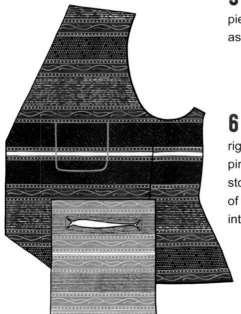

7 Turn the pocket to the wrong side of the waistcoat front, through the opening you have just cut. The pocket and waistcoat are now wrong sides together. Press the pocket opening. On the right side of the waistcoat, stitch close to the edge around the welt to hold it in place.

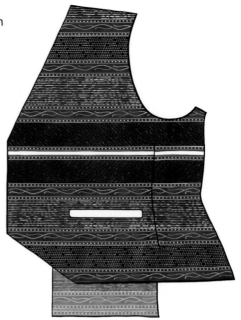

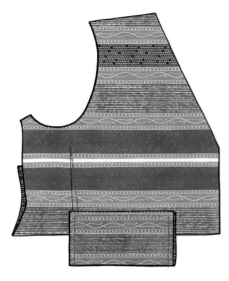

8 On the wrong side of the waistcoat front, fold the pocket in half and sew around the three raw edges. Make sure you fold the waistcoat out of the way so you are only sewing the pocket.

9 Place the main and lining patch pocket pieces together with the right sides facing. Sew around all the edges, leaving a 1in (2.5cm) gap on one of the straight lower sides (see step 5 on page 62). Clip the corners and curves (see pages 114–115).

10 Turn the pocket piece to the right side through the gap, and press. Topstitch (see page 106) along the top edge using a ⅛in (3mm) seam allowance. Pin the patch pocket to the left waistcoat front and stitch it in place close to the edge of the pocket. Leave the top of the pocket open and backstitch at the start and finish. Reinforce the top two pocket corners (see page 111).

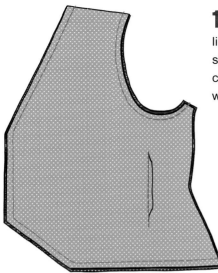

11 Place one of the waistcoat front pieces and waistcoat front lining pieces together with the right sides facing. Stitch around all sides except the shoulder and side seams. Clip the corners and curves. Turn right side out and press. Repeat with the second waistcoat front and waistcoat front lining pieces.

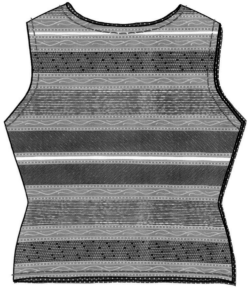

12 Place the waistcoat back and waistcoat back lining pieces together with the right sides facing. Stitch around all the sides except the shoulder and side seams. Clip the curves and corners. Turn right side out and press.

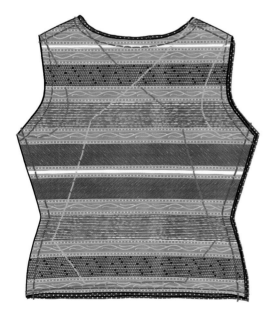

13 With the waistcoat fronts right side out, place each one inside the waistcoat back piece. Match the side and shoulder seams. Stitch across the shoulder and side seams, through all four layers of the waistcoat. The yellow and blue outlines in the illustration show how the fronts are placed inside the waistcoat back pieces.

14 Turn the waistcoat to the right side by pulling the fronts and back out through the gap in the back lining. Press the waistcoat. Slip stitch the opening in the back lining closed (see page 105). Topstitch all around the front and lower edges, and around the armholes. Make buttonholes on the left-hand side (when worn) of the waistcoat before sewing corresponding buttons on the right-hand side (see pages 118–119).

Rachel Romper

A romper is a versatile piece of clothing that is perfect for young girls who love to run, jump, and play. With this pattern, you can create a cute and comfortable item that your little girl will adore.

DIFFICULTY RATING ◎◎◎

SIZES
3–6 mth, 6–9 mth, 9–12 mth, 12–18 mth, 18–24 mth

FINISHED MEASUREMENTS
See page 123

MATERIALS AND TOOLS
1yd (1m) fabric, 45in (112cm) or 60in (152cm) wide
1 fat quarter fusible interfacing
2yd (2m) of ½in (1.3cm) wide bias binding
Matching sewing thread
6 x ½in (1.3cm) wide snaps/poppers
Sewing kit (see pages 100–101)

NOTES
All seam allowances are ⅜in (1cm) unless otherwise stated.

PATTERN PIECES REQUIRED
Front
Back
Ruffle
Crotch Band

1 Pre-wash and "press" your fabric before cutting and sewing (see page 9). Cut out the pattern pieces. Transfer all pattern markings to the pieces (see page 104).

2 Lay the front piece onto the back piece with the right sides together. Stitch the side seams. Finish the seams with zigzag stitch (see page 113) or an overlocker.

3 Take one front ruffle piece. Fold it along the center line with the right sides together and press. Stitch the straight short end.

4 Turn the ruffle to the right side. Stitch two lines of gathering stitches along the open curve, leaving thread tails at either end. Pull on either ends of the bobbin thread, until the gathered side is about 4½in (11.5cm), to create gathers in the fabric. Press the ruffle. Repeat with the other ruffle pieces.

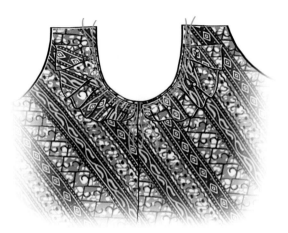

5 Pin a front ruffle piece to one front shoulder, with the smaller point of the ruffle positioned at the side seam. Pin a back ruffle piece to the back shoulder, again with the smaller point of the ruffle positioned at the side seam. Sew the ruffles in place. Repeat on the other side, with the remaining front and back ruffle pieces.

6 On the wrong side of the fabric, follow the manufacturer's instructions to apply the small interfacing pieces to the tops of the shoulders, in between the notches and upper edge. Turn the top of each shoulder edge toward the wrong side by ¼in (6mm) and press. Turn the edge over to the wrong side again so that it lines up with the fold line and notch. Topstitch (see page 106) each shoulder close to the fold line edge, next to notches.

7 Follow step 4 to gather the neckline on the front romper piece, in between the dots.

8 Finish the neckline and shoulders with bias binding (see page 117). Following the manufacturer's instructions, attach snap closures to the shoulders, using the pattern markings for placement. Attach the top halves of the snaps to the front, and the bottom halves of the snaps to the back. Alternatively, you can sew buttonholes on the front shoulder edges, and sew buttons on back shoulder edges (see pages 118–119).

9 Apply interfacing to the two crotch band pieces. Fold one band along the fold line with the right sides together. Stitch across both ends using a ⅝in (1.5cm) seam allowance. Trim each seam allowance in half. Repeat for the second crotch band piece.

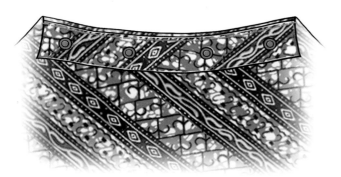

10 Turn each crotch band to the right side and press. Pin one of the crotch bands to the front crotch, with the right sides together. Line up the raw edges, and stitch together. Finish the raw edge with zigzag stitch or an overlocker. Repeat to sew the second crotch band to the back crotch. Press each crotch seam allowance away from the edge of the crotch. Attach snaps (or buttons and buttonholes) evenly spaced along each crotch band. Attach the top halves of the snaps to the front crotch band and the bottom half of snaps to the back band to match.

11 Sew two lines of gathering stitches (see step 4) in between the dots on the leg holes. Pull on both ends of the bobbin threads, to gather each leg. Attach bias binding to finish each leg hole.

This pattern is perfect for creating a fun and twirly skirt that your little girl will love. With the different panels, you can customize it to your heart's content. The circular design adds a playful element, making it perfect for a variety of occasions from dress-up to dance class.

Gabrielle Circle Skirt

DIFFICULTY RATING ◎ ◎ ◎

SIZES
2–3 yr, 3–4 yr, 4–5 yr

FINISHED MEASUREMENTS
See page 123

MATERIALS AND TOOLS
1yd (1m) fabric, 45in (112cm) wide
or ⅝yd (60cm) fabric, 60in (152cm)
wide, for the sides and waistband
⅝yd (60cm) contrast fabric, 45in
(112cm) or 60in (152cm) wide,
for the front and back
Matching sewing thread
24in (61cm) of 1in (2.5cm)
wide elastic
Safety pin
Sewing kit (see pages 100–101)

NOTES
All seam allowances are ⅜in (1cm)
unless otherwise stated.

PATTERN PIECES REQUIRED
Side
Front/Back
Waistband

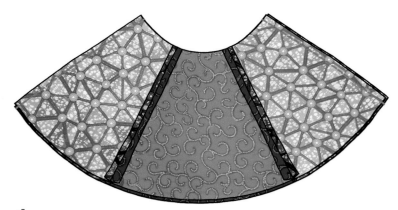

1 Pre-wash and "press" your fabric before cutting and sewing (see page 9). With the right sides together, pin two of the side pieces to the front piece, matching up the notches and lining up the raw edges. Stitch. Press the seams open. Repeat to sew the other two side pieces to the back piece. You now have one front skirt and one back skirt. Place these pieces together with the right sides facing, then stitch the front skirt to the back skirt along the two side seams.

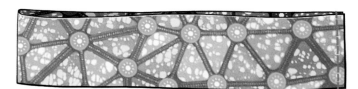

2 Fold the waistband piece in half with the right sides together. Line up the short ends and stitch them together. This is the side seam of the waistband.

3 Gather or ease (see pages 108 or 110) the top of the skirt into the waistband with the right sides together, and matching the seam of the waistband with one of the side seams of the skirt. Line up the raw edges and pin the edge of the waistband to the upper edge of the skirt. Stitch together along the top edge.

4 Press the waistband and its seam away from the skirt. Turn the upper edge of the waistband to its wrong side by ¼in (6mm) and press. Turn under this edge to the wrong side again, encasing the seam made in the previous step. Press and pin in place. On the right side of the skirt, topstitch close to the waistband seam, leaving a 2in (5cm) gap. Alternatively, you can topstitch in the ditch (see page 106), again leaving a 2in (5cm) gap.

5 Cut the 1in (2.5cm) wide elastic so that it measures the circumference of the child's waist minus 2in (5cm). Pin a safety pin on to one end of the elastic. Insert the elastic into the gap (see step 3 on page 92), gathering as you do so until the safety pin comes out through the other side of the gap. Stitch the ends of elastic together to secure, using several rows of zigzag stitches (see step 3 on page 59). Stitch the gap in the waistband closed.

6 Hem the skirt by turning the bottom edge under to the wrong side by ½in (1.3cm) and then by ½in (1.3cm) again. Topstitch the hem ⅜in (1cm) from the lower folded edge.

Raven Three-Tiered Skirt

✳ ✳

Create a beautiful and charming skirt that a little girl will adore. The
fabric used here is a patchwork print but you could have lots of fun
using a different fabric for each tier for a really dramatic effect.

DIFFICULTY RATING

MATERIALS AND TOOLS
Fabric—see step 1 for
amount required
Matching sewing thread
24in (61cm) of 1in (2.5cm)
wide elastic
Safety pin
Sewing kit (see pages 100–101)

NOTES
All seam allowances are ⅜in (1cm)
unless otherwise stated.

1 This is a no-pattern project. Simply measure the child's waist
circumference, decide how long you would like the skirt to be,
and plot those measurements into the calculations below
to work out how much fabric you will need. The width of each
tier ranges from 1.5 times to 2 times the waist measurement,
to create the gathered effect. Tier 1 is longer than the other
two tiers because this tier includes the waistband.

To calculate the length and width of each tier:

Tier 1:
Width = 1.5 x Waist measurement
Length = ⅓ Skirt length + 2½in (6.5cm) (for the waistband) +
¾in (2cm) (for the seam allowance)

Tier 2:
Width = 1.75 x Waist measurement
Length = ⅓ Skirt length + ¾in (2cm)

Tier 3:
Width = 2 x Waist measurement
Length = ⅓ skirt length + ¾in (2cm)

Once you have calculated the total amount of fabric you need,
pre-wash and "press" your fabric before cutting the piece for
each tier (see 9).

2 Fold the top tier in half with the right sides together, lining up the short sides. Stitch the short sides together. Press the seam open and finish using zigzag stitch (see page 113) or an overlocker. Repeat with the other two tiers.

3 Follow step 1 on page 108 to sew gathering stitches at the top edge of tier 3.

4 Turn tier 2 to the right side and place it inside tier 3, so that the right sides are together and the bottom edge of tier 2 is aligned with the top edge of tier 3. Follow steps 2–6 on pages 108–109 to gather the top edge of tier 3 into the bottom edge of tier 2 and then stitch together. Finish the seam (see page 114) and press tier 2 and its seam it away from tier 3.

5 Repeat step 4, this time gathering the top of tier 2 into the bottom edge of tier 1 and stitching them together. Press tier 1 and its seam away from tier 2.

6 Turn the skirt upper edge to the wrong side by ¼in (6mm) and then again by 1½in (4cm) to the wrong side. Pin in place and press. Stitch in place, 1¼in (3cm) away from the top folded edge, leaving a 2in (5cm) gap. Cut the piece of 1in (2.5cm) wide elastic so that it measures the circumference of the child's waist minus 2in (5cm). Pin a safety pin onto one end of your elastic (see step 3 on page 92). Insert the elastic into the gap, gathering as you do so, until the safety pin comes out through the other side of the gap. Stitch the ends of elastic together to secure, using several rows of zigzag stitches (see step 3 on page 59). Stitch the gap in the waistband closed.

7 Hem the skirt by turning the bottom edge under to the wrong side by ½in (1.3cm) and then by ½in (1.3cm) again. Topstitch the hem ⅜in (1cm) away from the lower folded edge.

With this pattern, you can create a charming and versatile dress that your little girl will love to wear. As well as being a fun and rewarding project, this pinafore dress will add a pop of color to a child's wardrobe.

Viola Pinafore Dress

DIFFICULTY RATING ◎◎◎

SIZES
2–3 yr, 3–4 yr, 4–5 yr

FINISHED MEASUREMENTS
See page 123

MATERIALS AND TOOLS
1½yd (1.4m) fabric, 45in (112cm)
or 60in (152cm) wide
20in (50cm) lightweight fusible
interfacing, , 45in (112cm) or
60in (152cm) wide
Matching sewing thread
2 x ½in (12mm) snaps/poppers
or buttons
Sewing kit (see pages 100–101)

NOTES
All seam allowances are ⅜in (1cm)
unless otherwise stated.

PATTERN PIECES REQUIRED
Front
Back
Back Facing
Front Facing

1 Prewash and "press" your fabric before cutting and sewing (see page 9). Transfer all pattern markings including the buttonhole markings even if you opt for snaps.

2 Staystitch the front and back neck edges. To staystitch, sew ¼in (6mm) from the raw edges (see page 111).

3 Stitch the front to the back along the side seams. Press the seams open and turn the dress inside out so the right side is on the outside.

4 Apply interfacing to the wrong side of each of the facing pieces. With right sides together, stitch these pieces together along their side seams. Press the seams open (see page 113).

5 With the right sides together, pin the facing to neck, shoulder, and armhole edges of the dress, matching the edges and side seams. Stitch the facing to the dress along the neck, shoulder and armhole edges.

6 Turn the facing to the inside of the dress. Press. Using a hand-sewing needle, tack the facings down to the side seams so that they will stay in place.

7 Using the markings on the pattern for the placement, attach the snaps using the manufacturer's instructions. The back shoulder pieces should overlap the front shoulders by 1in (2.5cm). Attach the bottoms of the snaps to the front shoulders of the dress, and the tops of the snaps to the back shoulders. If you are using buttons, sew buttonholes onto the back shoulders and buttons onto the front shoulders (see pages 118–119).

8 Hem the pinafore by turning the bottom edge to the wrong side by ½in (1.3cm) and then by ½in (1.3cm) again. Topstitch the hem ⅜in (1cm) from the lower folded edge.

Grace Simple Skirt

This easy-to-make skirt is a great project for beginners or anyone looking for a quick sewing project. The elasticated waistband provides comfort and adjustability, making it ideal for growing girls and easy to slip on and off.

DIFFICULTY RATING ◎◎◎

MATERIALS AND TOOLS

Fabric—see step 1 for amount required

Matching sewing thread

24in (61cm) of 1in (2.5cm) wide elastic

Safety pin

Sewing kit (see pages 100–101)

NOTES

All seam allowances are ⅜in (1cm) unless otherwise stated.

1 This is another no-pattern project. Measure the child's waist circumference, decide how long you would like the skirt to be, and plot those measurements into the calculations below to work out how much fabric you will need.

Length = Skirt length + 3in (8cm) (for the hem and waistband)
Width = 2 x Waist measurement + 1in (3cm)

Once you have calculated how much fabric you need in total, pre-wash and "press" your fabric before cutting and sewing (see page 9).

2 Fold the fabric in half with the right sides together, lining up the short sides of the rectangle. Stitch the short sides together. Press the seam open.

3 Turn under the skirt upper edge by ¼in (6mm) to the wrong side and press. Turn this edge to the wrong side again by 1½in (4cm) and press. Pin and then stitch close to the lower folded edge, leaving a 2in (5cm) gap. This is the casing for the elastic. Cut the piece of 1in (2.5cm) wide elastic so that it measures the circumference of the child's waist minus 2in (5cm). Pin a safety pin on to one end of your elastic. Insert the elastic into the gap and thread it through the casing, gathering as you do so until the safety pin comes out through the other side.

4 Make sure that the elastic is not twisted inside the casing. Stitch the ends of elastic together to secure, using several rows of zigzag stitches (see step 3 on page 59). Stitch the gap in the waistband closed.

5 Hem the skirt by turning the bottom edge to the wrong side by ½in (1.3cm) and then turning it to the wrong side again by ½in (1.3cm). Press. Topstitch (see page 106) the hem ⅜in (1cm) from the lower folded edge.

Zara A-line Dress

This timeless dress features a fitted bodice and a flared skirt.
You could use the pocket piece from the Adora Dress to add pockets.
Opt for buttons, poppers, or any closure of your choice.

DIFFICULTY RATING ◎◎◎

SIZES
2–3 yr, 3–4 yr, 4–5 yr

FINISHED MEASUREMENTS
See page 123

MATERIALS AND TOOLS
1yd (1m) fabric, 45in (112cm)
or 60in (152cm) wide
Matching sewing thread
42in (107cm) bias binding
11 x ½in (12mm) snaps/poppers
or buttons
Sewing kit (see pages 100–101)

NOTES
All seam allowances are ⅜in (1cm)
unless otherwise stated.

PATTERN PIECES REQUIRED
Front
Back

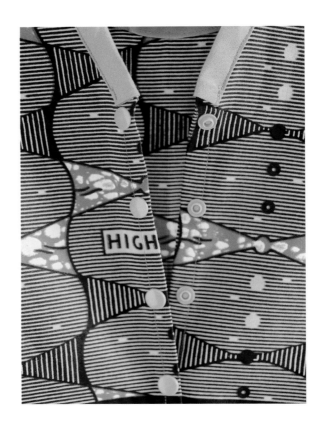

1 Pre-wash and "press" your fabric before cutting and sewing (see page 9).

2 Place the front pieces onto the back piece with the right sides together. Line up and pin the pieces together along the side seams and shoulder seams. Sew the pieces together at the side seams and shoulder seams. Press and finish the seams (see page 113).

3 Turn under one of the center fronts of the dress to the wrong side by ⅜in (1cm) and press. Turn it under to the wrong side again by ½in (1.2cm) and press. Topstitch in place close to the inside folded edge to make the placket (stand) for the snaps (or buttons and buttonholes, if using). Repeat on the other center front of the dress. If you are attaching snaps, you will attach the bottom halves of the snaps to the left-hand side of the dress (when worn) and the top halves to the right-hand side. Follow the manufacturer's instructions to attach the first snap piece to one side of the dress, 1½in (4cm) away from the lower edge of the dress. Space the remaining snap pieces ¾in (2cm) apart from each other. Repeat to attach the matching snap pieces on the other side of the dress. If you are sewing on buttons and buttonholes, space them out in the same way, sewing the buttons to the left-hand side edge (when worn) and the buttonholes to the right-hand side edge (see pages 118–119).

4 To hem the dress, turn the bottom edge under by ⅜in (1cm) and press. Turn it to the wrong side by ⅜in (1cm) again and press. Topstitch the hem close to the upper folded edge.

5 Finish raw edges of sleeve and neckline using bias binding (see page 117).

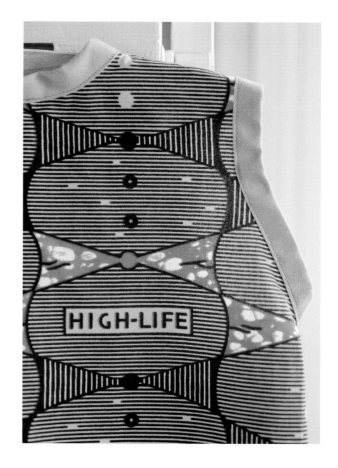

Make bedtime extra cozy with this child's pajama sewing pattern.
Designed to be comfortable and practical, this project is perfect
for creating sleepwear that your child will love to wear.

Vanessa Pajama Trousers

DIFFICULTY RATING ◎◎◎

SIZES
2–3 yr, 3–4 yr, 4–5 yr

FINISHED MEASUREMENTS
See page 123

MATERIALS AND TOOLS
1yd (1m) fabric, 45in (112cm)
or 60in (152cm) wide
Matching sewing thread
24in (61cm) of 1in (2.5cm)
wide elastic
Short length of ribbon or a label
Safety pin
Sewing kit (see pages 100–101)

NOTES
All seam allowances are ⅜in (1cm)
unless otherwise stated.

PATTERN PIECES REQUIRED
Front/Back

1 Pre-wash and "press" your
fabric before cutting and sewing
(see page 9). Fold each trouser
piece so that the right sides are
together and the bottom hem
and inside leg edges are lined
up. Stitch the inside leg seams.
Press and finish the seams using
a zigzag stitch (see page 113)
or an overlocker.

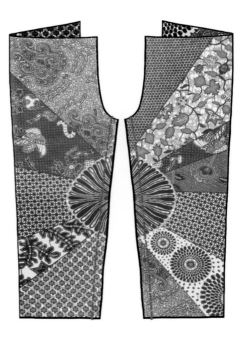

2 Turn one of the leg pieces right side
out. Insert the leg piece that is right
side out into the other leg piece so
that the right sides are facing. Line up
upper edges, crotch curves and inside
leg seams. Pin. Sew along the crotch
curve. Press and finish the seams.

3 Turn both legs right side out. Cut the piece of 1in (2.5cm) wide elastic so that it measures the circumference of the child's waist minus 2in (5cm).

4 Turn under the top edge of the pajama trousers by ¼in (6mm) to the wrong side and press. Turn this edge over to the wrong side again by 1½in (4cm). Press and pin in place. Stitch around this edge, 1¼in (3cm) away from the top folded edge and leaving a 2in (5cm) gap. Pin a safety pin on to one end of your elastic. Insert the elastic into the gap (see step 3 on page 92), gathering as you do so until the safety pin is out through the other side. Stitch the ends of elastic together to secure, using several rows of zig-zag stitches (see step 3 on page 59). Stitch the gap in the waistband closed.

5 Sew in a piece of ribbon or a label to the inside of the back of the pajama trousers, on or close to the waistband, to distinguish the front from the back. Hem the bottom of each trouser leg by turning it under to the wrong side by ½in (1.3cm) and then by ½in (1.3cm) again. Topstitch ⅜in (1cm) from the lower folded edge.

Sewing Kit

Here you'll find a guide to all the tools you will need to make the projects in this book.

▼▼▼

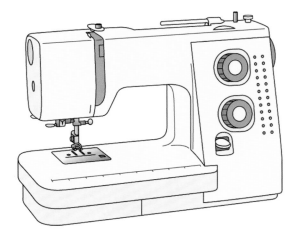

Sewing machine

There are many different brands of sewing machines to choose from, each offering a wide range of stitch options. For basic dressmaking, the stitches you will use the most are straight stitch (for sewing seams) and zigzag (for finishing edges and also for working buttonholes). If purchasing a new machine, look for one that sits firmly on a table. You'll find portable versions useful and easier to set up and put away.

Machine needles

Make sure you pick the right type for your machine, and remember, the lower the number, the thinner and finer the needle. A standard size 14 (90) needle is best for medium-weight fabrics including African wax print. A size 10 (70) needle is suitable for lightweight fabrics, while size 16 (100) is good for thick, heavy fabrics.

Overlocker

An overlocker (also known as a serger) is a type of sewing machine that is used to neaten seams and raw edges of fabric. It trims the fabric and uses multiple threads to enclose the edge, creating a neat and professional-looking finish. If you do a lot of sewing an overlocker can be a useful machine to invest in, but it's not essential as you can use the zigzag stitch on your sewing machine to neaten raw edges instead (see page 113).

Tape measure

This is essential for most measuring jobs, from taking body measurements to lining up all your pattern pieces on the fabric or measuring hems and buttonholes. Buy one in a flexible, non-fraying material that has metal ends and is numbered on both sides. Remember, a cheap tape measure may not be accurate.

Dressmaker's shears

Dressmaker's shears have handles that will take the thumb on one side and three fingers on the other. They are more heavily made than scissors and have bent handles that allow the fabric to lie flat on the table while you are cutting out your pattern pieces. Go for the best quality you can afford, with blades that are at least 7–8in (18–20cm) long. Treat your shears well and never use them for cutting anything other than fabric. Cutting paper with them will blunt them very quickly, and dropping them can easily put them out of alignment and damage the points.

Small, pointed scissors

A sharp pair of pointed scissors, with blades that are no more than 3in (7.5cm) long, is useful for trimming and clipping seams and cutting thread ends after stitching.

Pins

Pins come in a range of lengths and sizes to suit different fabric types. For general sewing, glass- or plastic-headed pins are the easiest to handle. Take care not to iron over plastic-headed pins as they will melt. Make sure that you buy plenty of them and store them in a pincushion to keep them safe and accessible.

Hand-sewing needles

Hand-sewing needles should be fine enough to slip through the fabric, yet strong enough not to break. The needles known as sharps are the most commonly used for hand sewing. They are available in a variety of sizes and points, numbered 1 to 12—unlike with machine needles, the larger number, the shorter and finer the needle. Size 9 is the most useful basic size for hand sewing.

Needle threader

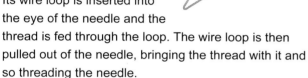

A needle threader makes it easy to thread hand needles and also machine needles. Its wire loop is inserted into the eye of the needle and the thread is fed through the loop. The wire loop is then pulled out of the needle, bringing the thread with it and so threading the needle.

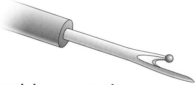

Quick unpick or seam ripper

This tool can be used to unpick incorrect stitches and seams quickly. It can also be used to cut the slits in buttonholes once they are stitched. You might find one of these included in your sewing machine accessories, but it will probably be small and difficult to hold, so buy one with a large handle. Remember, seam rippers can be dangerous so keep the top on and keep them away from children.

Thimble

You may not think a thimble is essential, but by the time you have stitched on a few buttons or sewn through some thick fabric by hand, you will very much want to use one! A thimble prevents your middle finger from being punctured when you are hand sewing. Find one that fits you comfortably and is made of metal, as plastic ones are liable to split.

Chalk markers

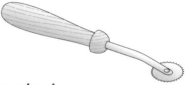

Chalk is ideal for marking around your pattern pieces onto fabric. It can be bought in wedge form, known as tailor's chalk, which is very economical; the edges can be sharpened with a knife. Alternatively, go for a chalk pencil, which is perfect for marking pocket positions, snap/popper positions or buttonholes, and the points of darts. Some chalk pencils have a brush attached, although marks are easily removed. Avoid wax, as it often leaves a greasy mark on your fabric, especially when melted with an iron, which you might find hard to remove.

Tracing wheel

This is a simple tool with multiple teeth on a wheel, attached to a handle; the teeth can be either serrated or smooth. It is used with dressmaker's carbon paper for transferring pattern markings, such as darts, onto the wrong side of fabric. Always place a piece of thick cardboard underneath the fabric to protect your work surface.

Dressmaker's carbon paper

This comes in packs containing two or more colors. It is placed ink side down onto the fabric. The pattern is then placed on top, and a tracing wheel is used to transfer the pattern markings to the fabric.

Steam iron and ironing board

Whether you are ironing out fabric creases or pressing seams, the combination of steam and heat is indispensable, so invest in a high-quality model that weighs at least 1lb (500g), because a lightweight portable one won't be good enough for pressing in folds or properly applying fusible interfacings. Choose an ironing board that's easy to adjust to the right height. You might find that lowering the board so that you can lean on the iron will make the process easier.

Techniques

Working with patterns and templates

The garment patterns on the pull-out sheets at the back of this book are printed to their actual size. You will need to trace them from the sheets onto tracing paper, greaseproof paper, or pattern paper, which is available from sewing and haberdashery stores. (Whatever you use, check that it is thin enough to see through.) Trace the pieces in the size that you need (the key on each pattern sheet shows you which line to follow) and cut them out.

On pages 120–121 you will find templates for the Joshua Messenger Bag and Ruby Head Tie. Simply photocopy or trace the templates and cut them out. Pin the photocopied template to your fabric (drawing around it if you wish), and then cut around it (or along the drawn line).

Positioning pattern pieces on the fabric

In dressmaking, the vast majority of pattern pieces need to be cut from a double layer of fabric. You generally have to fold your fabric in a particular way before you pin the pattern pieces to it and cut them out. There are three main ways of folding the fabric (see right).

Many pattern pieces are symmetrical—the front of a bodice or the back of a shirt, for example. Instead of being cut as one huge paper pattern, these pieces are often cut out as a half piece and the center line is placed on the fold of the fabric. A double-headed arrow on a pattern indicates an edge that has to be placed on the fold.

Sometimes you may have two pieces that are the same shape but need to be mirror images of each other—the left and right sides of a shirt front, for example, or left and right sleeves. If you're cutting these from a doubled layer of fabric, there's no problem—the two pieces will automatically be mirror images when they're cut out. But if you're cutting them from a single layer of fabric, you must remember to flip the pattern over before you cut out the second piece so that you get a left- and a right-hand piece.

Fold the fabric, then pin the pattern pieces in place and either draw around them with tailor's chalk and cut out, or simply cut around the pattern pieces. Lay out all the pattern pieces on your fabric before you begin cutting to make sure you're using the most economical layout and avoid wasting fabric. If you're using a print and want to match the pattern across two adjoining pieces, you may also find that you need to move the pieces around slightly to get the best result.

Fold in half widthwise, matching up the selvages.

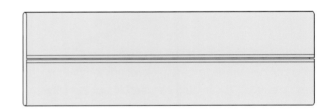

Fold both selvages in to meet the center.

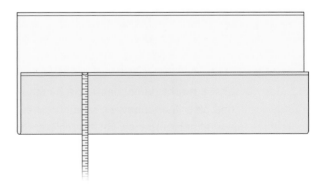

Fold one or both selvages in toward the center, just far enough to accommodate the pattern piece(s).

Pattern matching

Often in dressmaking you are advised to follow the straight grain when cutting out your pattern pieces in your fabric. However, with African wax print fabrics you should follow the design. This will mean cutting on either the straight grain or the cross grain, depending on the most pleasing direction of the print. For more information on pattern matching African wax print fabrics, see pages 10–11.

Pattern matching by eye takes time and experience. Play around with the paper pattern pieces and your fabric, while at the same time trying to picture how the finished garment will look. Take your time—pattern placement often takes longer than the actual sewing but once cut, and the pattern placement is correct, the sewing can be straightforward. The methods below can help when pattern matching with non-directional or detailed designs and will depend on whether you are cutting out from a single layer or double (on the fold).

Tracing and cutting the design

1 Cut out a copy of the pattern piece in pattern paper.

2 Lay your fabric out flat in a single layer. Place the copied pattern paper over key pieces, such as center fronts or backs, and cut out one piece.

3 With the paper pattern still attached, trace the outline of the main elements of the fabric design with a soft pencil.

4 Match the tracing to the fabric pattern to cut out a matching second piece, remembering to flip the pattern if you need a mirrored piece. Match seamlines.

Cutting double

1 Fold your fabric in half and match the selvages, checking that the pattern is matched along the edges.

2 Place the paper pattern aligned with an element of the design, using pins through the two layers at key elements of the design. Lift the edge to check that the pin marks the same design underneath.

3 Pin the fabric edges so that they won't move, and cut out the two layers on the fold.

▼▼▼

Pattern marks for cutting out

Grain lines
These lines indicate where the grain line (or direction of the fabric) should be when that pattern piece is cut out in fabric. These marks don't need to be transferred onto your fabric; however, you do need to pay attention to them as they tell you how to position the pattern piece in relation to the straight grain in your fabric (but see also Pattern Matching, above).

Place to fold line
When the grain line turns in at each end at right angles, it means that the edge of the pattern that the arrows point to needs to be placed on a lengthwise fold in the fabric. You cut around all other sides of the pattern except this one on the fold and you will end up with one big symmetrical fabric piece once the pattern is cut out.

Transferring pattern marks to the fabric

Patterns are also marked to show where to position features like pockets, buttonholes, and other fastenings, or where you need to place darts or pleats. Transfer any markings to the fabric before you unpin the pattern pieces. You can do this with either a chalk pencil, carbon paper, or tailor's tacks (see page 105), or by using scissors to make notches in the fabric. If your fabric is folded, push a pin straight down through the fabric at the marked point, and then mark the position on the bottom layer of fabric.

Notches are found on the edge of patterns on seam lines, and are used to help you match up seams and join the correct pieces together.

▼▼▼

Interfacing

Interfacing is a special type of fabric applied to the inside of a garment to strengthen specific parts, such as collars, cuffs, and buttonholes. Interfacings come in several weights and degrees of crispness and can be woven or non-woven, sew-in or fusible (iron-on). With such a wide range available it is possible to find an interfacing suitable for every type of fabric. If you are unsure which is best for your fabric, ask the salesperson for a recommendation.

Applying fusible (iron-on) interfacing

Fusible interfacings are the easiest to use and are the ones that we recommend for the projects in this book. They have heat-sensitive glue on one side; the manufacturer normally provides instructions for your iron heat setting on the ends of the interfacing rolls, but this information may also be printed down the edges of the interfacing itself.

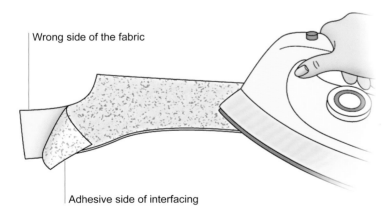

Wrong side of the fabric

Adhesive side of interfacing

Lay the cut interfacing pieces adhesive side down on the wrong side of the garment pieces. To fix the interfacing in position, set your iron to a steam setting following the manufacturer's instructions, then place the iron firmly on it for a few seconds at a time. Lift the iron and reposition it; do not slide the iron across, as this could move the interfacing and cause creases. Allow the interfacing to cool. Check that it is fused all over and re-press any loose areas. Continue stitching your garment together as normal.

Hand stitches

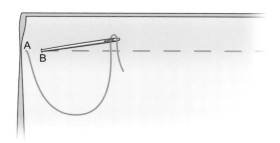

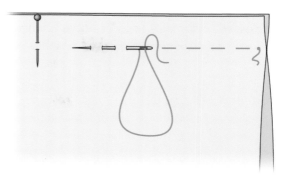

Securing with backstitch

Bring the needle and thread to the upper side of the fabric at A. Insert the needle through all the fabric layers at B, one stitch length behind A, and bring it back up again at A. Repeat to form another backstitch in the same place. Trim the thread end.

Basting (tacking)

Working from right to left, take evenly spaced stitches about ¼in (6mm) long through the fabric layers, sewing close to the seamline but within the seam allowance. Take several stitches onto your needle at one time, before drawing the thread through the fabric.

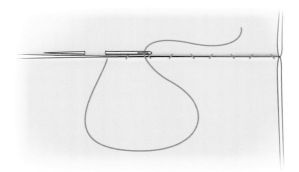

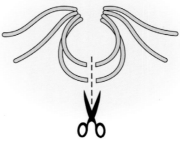

Slip stitch

This is a hand stitch worked to close gaps in seams. Bring the needle out through the seam allowance to hide the knot in the seam. Take the needle across to the other seam, picking up a few threads and emerging approximately ⅛in (3mm) along. Take the needle back to the opposite side, then repeat, working across seam and pulling the thread to join the two sides.

Tailor's tacks

To work a tailor's tack, thread the needle with a double loop of cotton in a contrasting color to your fabric, but do not knot the ends. At the marked point on the pattern, take the needle down through the fabric and back up again to the right side, and then repeat the process through the same stitch to leave a loop on the surface of the fabric. Leave a tail of thread on each side and do not draw the loop tight. When you remove the paper pattern, the tack will remain on the surface of the right side of the fabric as a position guide. If the tailor's tack is worked over two layers of fabric, gently pull the layers apart and cut through the threads of the loop in the center; this will leave the threads of the tack stitching on both pieces of fabric.

Machine stitches

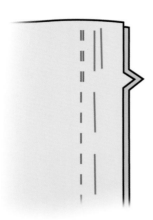

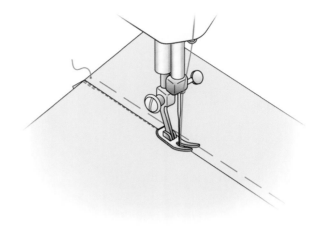

Backstitch

A short length of reverse stitching at the beginning and end of a row of straight stitching, made by using the reverse lever on the sewing machine. This secures the stitches and gives extra strength to the seam.

Stitch-in-the-ditch

A row of straight stitching made very close to a seam on the right side, so that it "sinks" into the seam groove. It is used to create a defined edge or to give an invisible finish, for example to hold a facing in place inside a neckline.

Topstitching

Topstitching is often done to finish an edge—as well as being decorative, it prevents the underside of the edge from rolling to the outside. Working from the right side, line up your finished seam edge on the chosen guideline and begin stitching, turning any corners by lifting your presser foot and pivoting your fabric around the needle. Trim your thread ends even with the raw edges.

Dressmaking techniques

Contour darts

These are long darts, which have a point at each end; they are often used on fitted and semi-fitted garments. The widest part of the dart fits into the waistline and then tapers off to fit the bust/chest and the hip, or the shoulder blades and hip. Contour darts are usually shown on patterns as a long, thin diamond, with stitching lines and a series of dots to be matched.

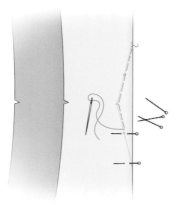

1 Transfer the dart markings to the wrong side of your fabric (see Transferring Pattern Marks to the Fabric, page 104). Working from the wrong side of the fabric, fold along the center of the dart. Match and pin the dots and stitching lines, first at the waist, then at the points, and then at any marks in between. Baste the dart in place just inside the stitching lines and remove the pins.

2 A contour dart is usually stitched in two halves, starting at the middle and stitching toward the point. Instead of reverse stitching to start, overlap the stitching at the middle. At each point, cut the thread ends, leaving at least 4in (10cm). Knot the ends together, but do not pull too tightly. Trim the thread ends to ⅜in (1cm).

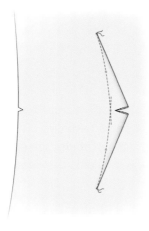

3 Remove the basting stitches and clip into the dart at the middle to within ⅛in (3mm) of the stitching line; this will allow for the dart to curve smoothly at the waist. Press the dart flat as it was stitched, then press it toward the center of the garment.

Gathers

Gathers are tiny, soft folds formed by drawing up fabric into a smaller area. It is best to form large areas of gathers by machine, as controlling the fullness evenly across the pieces is easier, but small sections can be gathered by hand if you prefer.

Machine gathering

Machine gathering is done by stitching two rows of long machine stitches along the edge to be gathered, within the seam allowances. The fabric is then gathered up by pulling on the bobbin threads.

1 Leaving long thread ends, work two parallel rows of gathering stitches 1/4in (6mm) apart within the seam allowance along your fabric edge, with the outer row of stitching a thread's width from the seamline. Do not stitch over seams—stitch between any seams where necessary.

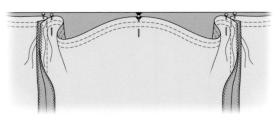

2 Divide the stitched edge and the edge to which it will be attached into four or more equal sections and mark them with a pin. With right sides together, pin the stitched edge to the other edge, matching marker pins. Match any corresponding pattern markings and seams.

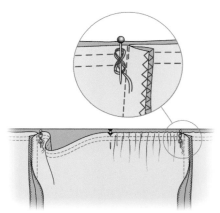

3 At one end, secure the bobbin threads by twisting them around a pin in a figure eight. At the other end, pull both bobbin threads together and gently ease the gathers along the threads. When the gathered edge fits the other piece, secure the thread ends around another pin, as before. On long edges, gather the fabric from each end toward the center, rather than trying to gather across the entire piece all at once.

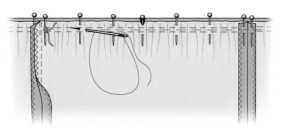

4 Unwind the thread ends from around each end pin, and knot each pair together to secure them; trim the ends to about 1in (2.5cm). With the gathered side on top, baste the two layers together between the two rows of stitching, using short stitches. Remove the pins.

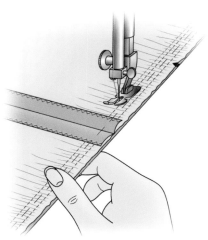

5 Return your machine stitch length and tension to the appropriate setting. With the gathered side on top, machine stitch the gathered edge to the corresponding edge, reverse stitching to start and finish. As you sew, hold the fabric on either side of the machine foot to prevent the gathers from being pushed and stitched into pleats. Remove the basting.

6 Diagonally trim crossed seam allowances as shown to reduce bulk. Using the tip of the iron, press the seam allowances flat as they were stitched, but do not press the gathers. Finish the seam allowances together. Open the sections out and press the seam toward the flat section. Press the gathers by sliding the point of the iron into the gathers toward the seam.

▼▼▼▼▼▼▼▼▼▼▼▼▼▼▼▼▼▼▼▼▼▼▼▼▼▼▼▼▼▼▼▼

MACHINE GATHERING TIPS

• Loosen the upper tension on the machine slightly so that the fabric will slide along the bobbin thread more easily.

• Set your machine to a longer stitch: 12 stitches per inch (2.0mm stitch length) for lightweight fabrics, to 6–7 stitches per inch (4.0mm stitch length) for heavier fabrics. Test the tension and stitch length on a scrap of the fabric first.

• Stitch from the right side of the fabric, so that the bobbin threads, which are pulled to form the gathers, will be easily accessible when you are working from the wrong side later, adjusting the gathers.

• Leaving long thread ends, stitch between any seams, keeping the seam allowances out of the way, because gathering does not work well through two layers of fabric.

▲▲▲▲▲▲▲▲▲▲▲▲▲▲▲▲▲▲▲▲▲▲▲▲▲▲▲▲▲▲▲▲

Hand gathering

You can also gather small sections by hand if you prefer; this is done using simple running stitch. Start by making several tiny backstitches (see page 105) to fasten the thread securely at one end of the section to be gathered. Sew a row of small, evenly spaced running stitches just above the seamline, then sew a second row of running stitches parallel to the first, just below the seamline. Pull up the two loose threads and distribute the fabric fullness evenly until the section measures the desired length. Anchor the loose threads around a pin at the finishing end (see Machine Gathering the Fabric, step 3, on page 108) and apply your gathered section as shown in steps 4, 5, and 6 (see page 108 and left).

Pivoting at a corner

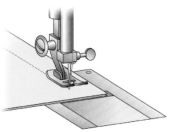

1 If there is no cornering crossline on your bobbin cover, stick a piece of masking tape the same distance in front of the needle hole as the depth of the seam allowance. Reverse stitching to start, stitch a ⅝in (1.5cm) seam toward the corner, stopping with the needle down in the fabric when the bottom edge of the fabric reaches the cornering crossline or edge of your tape. Raise the machine foot.

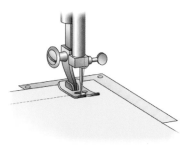

2 Pivot the fabric on the needle through 90 degrees, bringing the bottom edge of the fabric in line with the ⅝in (1.5cm) guideline on the needle plate. Lower the foot and continue stitching to the end of the seam, reverse stitching to finish.

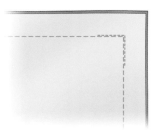

3 Strengthen the corner by reinforcing it with a row of small stitches, about 12 stitches per inch (2.0mm stitch length), extending ¾in (2cm) either side of the corner, stitching and pivoting accurately on top of the existing stitching line.

Understitching

Understitching, like topstitching, is done from the right side of the fabric. It is stitched close to the seamline and its purpose is to keep facings and seams lying flat and in a particular direction.

With the right side of the facing on top, topstitch close to the seamline, stitching through the facing and the seam allowances at the same time.

Ease stitching

On some garments you may be required to do ease stitching, which provides a bare amount of fullness, called ease, at a place where it is needed. It is worked in the same way as machine gathering (see page 108), but the stitch length is set to about 9 stitches per inch (3.0mm stitch length), and the stitches are drawn up just enough to pull in the fibers of the fabric to fit a smaller area, without forming any puckers or gathers.

Staystitching

This is a row of machine stitching that is worked on the cut garment pieces before you start to sew them together. It is used on curved and bias seams such as necklines and waist edges, to stop them from stretching while you are sewing the garment.

Machine stitch a row of medium-length straight stitches just inside the seam allowance of your cut piece. Lay the cut piece back on your pattern to double-check that it is still the same size and shape. Continue sewing the garment.

Reinforcing pocket corners

Pockets normally get a lot of strain as you push your hands in and out. It is therefore advisable to reinforce the corners to give them more strength.

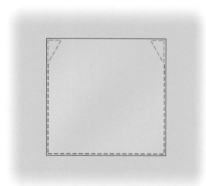

Stitched triangles

At each top corner, topstitch close to the edge for about ¼in (6mm) along the top edge and then diagonally down to the side edge, forming a small triangle at each corner.

Making a shirt collar

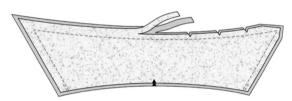

1 With right sides together, pin the collar pieces together along the side and upper edges, then machine stitch along these edges, taking the appropriate seam allowance. Trim the seam allowance in half, and notch the curve and trim the corners (see pages 114 and 115). Using the corner of your ironing board, press the seam open (see page 113) and then toward the interfaced portion.

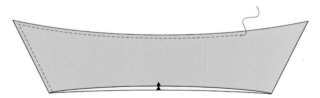

2 Turn the collar right side out, carefully pushing the corners out to form neat points. Working from the interfaced side, press the seamed edges flat and topstitch the finished edges if desired (see page 106).

Finishing techniques

Pressing seams open
Run the tip of an iron along the seam so the two edges of fabric open out to lie flat on either side of the seam.

Zigzag stitch
This machine stitch is the fastest way to finish a raw edge, leaving it neat and flat. As well as seam allowances, it is suitable for other raw edges, such as hem or facing edges. Use an overcasting foot if your machine has one, to achieve the smoothest zigzag stitch; this foot has a special pin over which the stitches are formed, stopping them from pulling up tight and creating a lumpy edge.

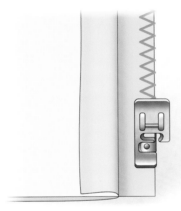

Plain zigzag using an overcasting foot
First trim the edges to remove any fraying, then refer to your instruction manual for the correct stitch settings. Place the edge of your fabric under the overcasting foot, with the pin, on the foot along the edge of the fabric, and stitch along the raw edge.

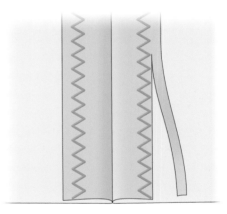

Plain zigzag using a normal zigzag foot
Using the normal zigzag foot, stitch on a scrap of your fabric before you begin, to double-check the stitch tension and make sure that it doesn't roll up the fabric edges. Set your stitch for a medium-width and short-length zigzag, then stitch ⅛in (3mm) from the edge of the seam allowance. Trim away the outer edge of the fabric, close to the zigzag stitching.

Neatening seam edges

Neatening seam edges prevents them from fraying, helps them lay flat, and gives a tidy, professional touch. There are many ways of doing this, but for a quick effective finish, you can machine overcast the edges using a zigzag stitch.

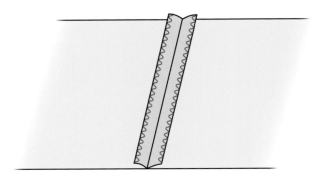

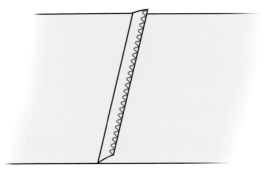

Open seam

Zigzag or overlock (serge) on the right side of both single edges of the seam to be joined. With right side together, stitch the seam using the required seam allowance. Press the seam allowances open on the wrong side.

Closed seam

With right sides together, stitch the seam using the required seam allowance. Zigzag or overlock the two raw edges together. On the wrong side, press the seam allowance to one side.

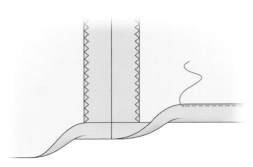

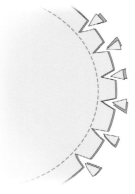

Double-turned hem

Double hemming gives a very neat finish and will prevent fraying. Following the measurements specified in the project, fold the edge of the fabric over to the wrong side and press. Fold over again, pin, baste (tack), press, and either topstitch (see page 106) in place from the right side or machine stitch from the wrong side, stitching as close as possible to the folded edge.

Clipping curved seam allowances

This helps curved seams lie flat and will make a real difference to the look of your finished project. Use the tips of your fabric scissors (don't use tiny embroidery scissors as this will dull the blades) to cut into the seam allowance after stitching, taking great care not to cut through any of the stitches. Seams that curve outward need wedge-shaped notches cut into the seam allowance, while for seams that will curve inward, little slits will do.

Trimming corners

For neat corners, you need to trim off the excess fabric across the point before you turn the project right side out, so that the finished corner is neat and square. Cut off the fabric across the corner about ⅛in (3mm) away from the stitching, taking care not to cut through the stitches.

Binding

Binding is used in several projects in this book. To bind straight edges, strips of fabric cut on the straight of grain can be used. To bind curves (around a neckline, for example), you will need to cut fabric strips on the bias.

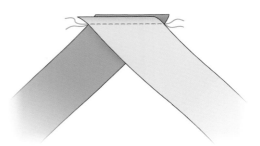

1 Take a square or rectangular piece of fabric, approximately the size of a fat quarter, and press it flat. Fold one corner of the fabric over until the side that is at right angles to the selvage is lined up with the selvage. The resulting fold line is the bias at 45 degrees to the selvage. Using a ruler and chalk, mark lines 2in (5cm) apart, following the 45-degree angle across the fabric.

2 Cut along these lines until you have enough strips to make the length you need to go around a hemline, sleeves, or neckline plus approximately 1in (2.5cm). To join strips together, cut the two ends that are to be joined at a 45-degree angle. Place one strip on top of the other, right sides together, and stitch the pieces together diagonally.

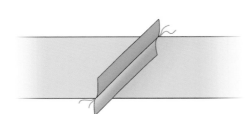

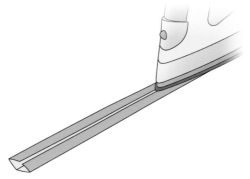

3 Press the seam open and trim the excess from the sides, in line with the edges of the strip. Continue to join the strips together until the bias strip is the length you need for your project.

4 With wrong sides together, fold the strip in half widthwise and press. Open out the central crease, then fold each long edge of the binding in to meet at the central crease and press again.

Attaching bias binding by machine

You can finish any fabric edge with binding.
Use store-bought or make your own (see opposite),
in either self-fabric or contrasting fabric.

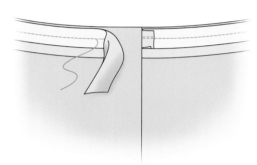

1 First one narrow side of the binding is applied to the
garment edge with right sides together. Start by opening
out the folds on the binding and turn back ⅜in (1cm) at
one end; align this with a garment seam if there is one.
With the long raw edge of the binding even with the raw
edge of the garment, pin the binding in place. Machine
stitch along the top fold line, reverse stitching at the
start, and finishing the stitching about 2in (5cm) from
the starting point.

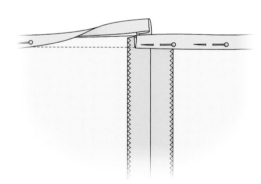

2 Trim away the excess binding, leaving ⅜in (1cm)
to overlap the turned-back starting end. Still following
the top fold line, stitch the remaining binding in place
through all layers. Trim the seam to reduce the bulk and
press the seam allowances toward the binding. Now
flip the opposite folded long edge of the binding over to
meet the seamline on the wrong side of the garment,
enclosing the raw edge of the garment. Pin in place and
then topstitch from the right side.

Buttons and buttonholes

Many modern sewing machines will stitch buttonholes automatically, but on older machines you may have to stitch them in stages. Check the manual for the correct foot and settings for your machine. Practice sewing your buttonholes first by making the correct length marks and stitching them on a double layer of scrap fabric.

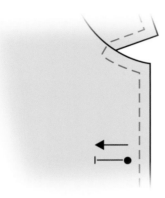

1 Mark the button positions from the pattern onto the overlapping side using tailor's chalk (right over left for women and girls and left over right for men and boys). Mark your buttonhole either vertically or horizontally, depending on the width of the button band.

2 Stitch the buttonholes on the right side of the garment; the bar tack ends should lie either side of the marks. Cut between the lines of stitches, snipping inward from each end to ensure accuracy. Pass the button through to ensure that the opening is the correct size.

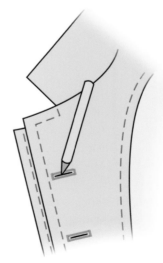

3 When all the buttonholes are stitched and cut, lay the two front edges right sides together. Mark through each buttonhole, at the end nearest the front edge, onto the underlapping side, to establish the button position. Sew the buttons at the marked positions.

Sewing on a button

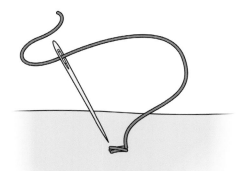

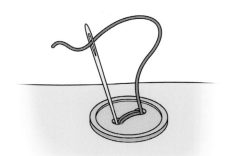

1 Mark the place where you want the button to go. Push the needle up from the back of the fabric and sew a few stitches over and over in this place.

2 Now bring the needle up through one of the holes in the button. Push the needle back down through the second hole and through the fabric. Bring it back up through the first hole. Repeat this five or six times. If there are four holes in the button, use all four of them to make a cross pattern. Make sure that you keep the stitches close together under the middle of the button.

3 Finish with a few small stitches over and over on the back of the fabric and trim the thread.

Hook-and-loop tape

To attach sew-on hook-and-loop tape, cut it to the required length and then pin and baste the hook side to the right side of the opening's underlap; the tape is tough, so use a thimble. Machine stitch the tape in place along both long edges and across the ends, overlapping the stitching to secure. Press the second side of the tape onto the first and then fold over the other side of the opening. Pin in place so that the tape is not visible from the right side. Separate the tapes, then baste and machine stitch in place, as before. Remove the basting and then hand stitch over the cut ends, sewing through one layer of fabric only.

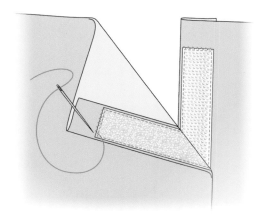

Templates

See page 102 for instructions on using templates.

Flap
Cut 2 on fold in fabric

Front/Back
Cut 4 on fold in fabric
(Or cut 2 on fold in fabric and cut 2 on fold in lining, if using a contrasting lining fabric.)

Joshua Messenger Bag

See page 32
Full size

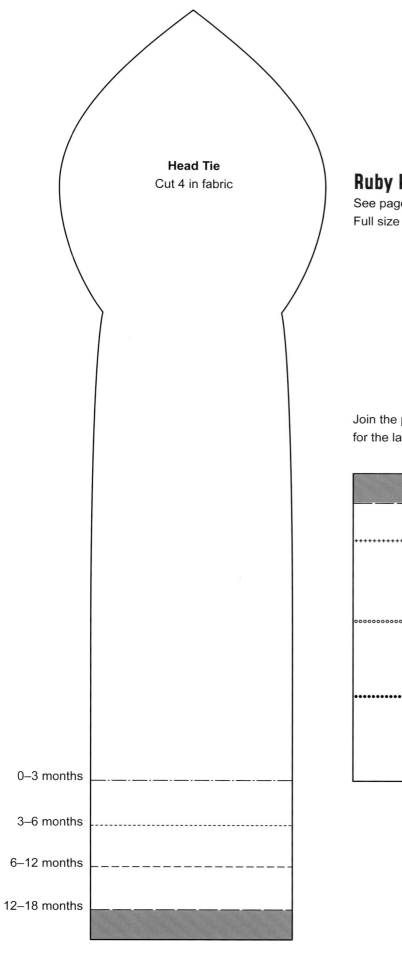

Head Tie
Cut 4 in fabric

Ruby Head Tie

See page 36
Full size

Join the pieces along the gray tabs
for the largest four sizes.

18–24 months

2–3 years

3–4 years

4–5 years

0–3 months

3–6 months

6–12 months

12–18 months

Measurements charts

▼▼

The garments and some of the accessories have pattern pieces for different sizes, which have been designed according to the following guide. Check these charts before you decide which size to make. If the child you're making the garment for is in between sizes, make the larger size.

Use the body measurement size chart as a starting point, but also consider the finished measurements charts. These give you the measurements each garment or accessory will be for each size once it is made. By comparing the measurements from the two charts, you will get an idea of how loose or fitted the garment is designed to be.

Body measurements

	0–3 months	3–6 months	6–9 months	9–12 months	12–18 months	18–24 months	2–3 years	3–4 years	4–5 years
Height	28in (71cm)	29½in (75cm)	30¼in (77cm)	31in (79cm)	33in (84cm)	35in (89cm)	38in (96.5cm)	41in (104cm)	43in (109cm)
Chest	18in (45.5cm)	19in (48.5cm)	19½in (49.5cm)	20in (51cm)	20½in (52cm)	21in (53.5cm)	22in (56cm)	23in (58.5cm)	24in (61cm)
Waist	18½in (47cm)	19in (48.5cm)	19¼in (49cm)	19½in (49.5cm)	19¾in (50cm)	20in (51cm)	20½in (52cm)	21in (53.5cm)	21½ (54.5cm)

Finished measurements

Nicole Baby Hat (see page 28)

	3–6 months	6–12 months	12–18 months
Head circumference	17in (43cm)	18in (45.5cm)	19in (48.5cm)

Ruby Head Tie (see page 36)

	0–3 months	3–6 months	9–12 months	12–18 months	18–24 months	2–3 years	3–4 years	4–5 years
Finished length (unstretched, before it is tied)	49cm	51cm	54cm	56cm	58cm	63cm	67cm	71cm

Billie Soft Crib Shoes (see page 38)

	0–3 months	3–6 months	6–9 months	9–12 months
Length	3½in (9cm)	4in (10cm)	4½in (11.5cm)	5in (12.5cm)

Amelia Bloomers (see page 56)

	6–9 months	9–12 months	12–18 months	18–24 months
Hip	26½in (67.5cm)	27¼in (69cm)	28in (71cm)	28¾in (73cm)

Sydney Shorts *(see page 58)*

	2–3 years	3–4 years	4–5years
Hip	27in (68.5cm)	28in (71cm)	29in (73.5cm)
Length from center back of waistline to hem	13⅜in (34cm)	14½in (37cm)	15¾in (40cm)

Adora Dress *(see page 60)*

	6–9 months	9–12 months	12–18 months	18–24 months
Chest	22½in (57cm)	23¼in (59cm)	24in (61cm)	24½in (62cm)
Waist	19in (48.5cm)	19¾in (50cm)	20½in (52cm)	20¾in (52.5cm)
Bodice length	7in (18cm)	7½in (19cm)	7¾in (19.5cm)	8¼in (21cm)
Skirt length	10½in (26.5cm)	11½in (29cm)	12¼in (31cm)	13in (33cm)

Stirling Shirt *(see page 64)*

	2–3 years	3–4 years	4–5years
Length from center back of neckline to hem	16½in (42cm)	17½in (44.5cm)	18¼in (46.5cm)

Zachary Waistcoat *(see page 70)*

	2–3 years	3–4 years	4–5years
Chest	22½in (57cm)	23¼in (59cm)	24in (61cm)

Rachel Romper *(see page 74)*

	3–6 months	6–9 months	9–12 months	12–18 months	18–24 months
Chest	26in (66cm)	26¾in (68cm)	27¾in (70.5cm)	28½in (72.5cm)	29¼in (74.5cm)
Hip	33½in (85cm)	34¾in (88.5cm)	36in (91.5cm)	37¼in (94.5cm)	38½in (98cm)

Gabrielle Circle Skirt *(see page 78)*

	2–3 years	3–4 years	4–5years
Waist	20½in (52cm)	21in (53.5cm)	21½in (54.5cm)
Hip	23in (58.4cm)	24in (61cm)	25in (63.5cm)
Finished length	11½in (29cm)	12in (30.5cm)	13½in (34.5cm)

Viola Pinafore Dress *(see age 86)*

	2–3 years	3–4 years	4–5years
Chest	22in (56cm)	23in (58.5cm)	24in (61cm)
Waist	20½in (52cm)	21in (53.5cm)	21½in (54.5cm)
Length from base of neckline to hem	19in (48.5cm)	20in (51cm)	21in (53.5cm)

Zara A-line Dress *(see page 93)*

	2–3 years	3–4 years	4–5years
Chest	28in (71cm)	28½in (72.5cm)	29in (73.5cm)
Length from base of neckline to hem	21¼in (54cm)	22¾in (58cm)	25¼in (64cm)

Vanessa Pajama Trousers *(see page 96)*

	2–3 years	3–4 years	4–5years
Hip	26in (66cm)	27in (68.5cm)	28in (71cm)
Length from center back of waistline to hem	21⅝in (55cm)	22¾in (58cm)	24¾in (63cm)

Suppliers and Resources

African wax print fabric retailers

Dovetailed
My own company, for online sales of African wax print fabric by the yard, fat quarters, patterns, sewing supplies, and haberdashery. Orders can be shipped worldwide.
dovetailed.co.uk

VLISCO
Online sales of African wax print fabric. Orders can be shipped worldwide.
vlisco.com

Manufacturers

Vlieseline
Interfacing. Store locator on website.
www.vlieseline.com

UK sewing and haberdashery retailers

John Lewis
Haberdashery and sewing supplies
www.johnlewis.com

Hobbycraft
www.hobbycraft.co.uk

William Gee Ltd
London, UK store and online sales.
www.williamgee.co.uk

US sewing and haberdashery retailers

Hobby Lobby
www.hobbylobby.com

JoAnn Fabrics and Craft Stores
www.joann.com

Michaels
www.michaels.com

Book
Anne Grosfilley, *African Wax Print Textiles* (Prestel, 2018)

Website
Wax Print Film
waxprintfilm.com

Index

Acknowledgments

It has been an honour to work on this book and I could not be prouder of this collection of garments, homewares, and accessories all sewn together in my favorite fabric: African wax print. It is always a joy seeing what the sewing community has been making with these fabrics, and I cannot wait to see all of your creations and pattern "hacks" using this book. Do share your makes using the hashtag #dovetailedlondon.

I would like to extend my thanks to Penny Craig, Jenny Dye, Sally Powell, Patricia Harrington, and all the team at CICO Books, and the editor Marie Clayton, designer Alison Fenton, photographer James Gardiner, and stylist Nel Haynes. It has been great to work with such a brilliant team!

Finally, to my husband, our three lovely children, and to my Mum, words alone cannot express how grateful I am to you all for your continued love and support.